NORTHERN LIGHT

This book is dedicated
to the memory of
David Jonathan Shapiro
1954 – 1985

Our hearts will always grieve
the premature farewell.

Published in the United States by Clarkson N. Potter, Inc.,
225 Park Avenue South, New York, New York 10003,
and distributed in Canada by the Canadian MANDA Group
Originally published in Sweden by Streiffert & Co., Bokförlag HB,
Karlavägen 71, Stockholm
CLARKSON N. POTTER, POTTER, and colophon are trademarks of
Clarkson N. Potter, Inc.

Manufactured in Sweden

Library of Congress Cataloging-in-Publication Data
Bjelke, Rolf.
Northern Light.
1. Northern Light (Ship) 2. Polar regions.
I. Shapiro, Deborah, 1951– . II. Title.
G587.B53 1986 919.8′04 86-12324
ISBN 0-517-56406-8

10 9 8 7 6 5 4 3 2 1
First American Edition

NORTHERN LIGHT

ONE
COUPLE'S
EPIC VOYAGE
FROM THE
ARCTIC
TO THE
ANTARCTIC

ROLF BJELKE & DEBORAH SHAPIRO

Clarkson N. Potter, Inc./Publishers NEW YORK

DISTRIBUTED BY CROWN PUBLISHERS, INC.

Contents

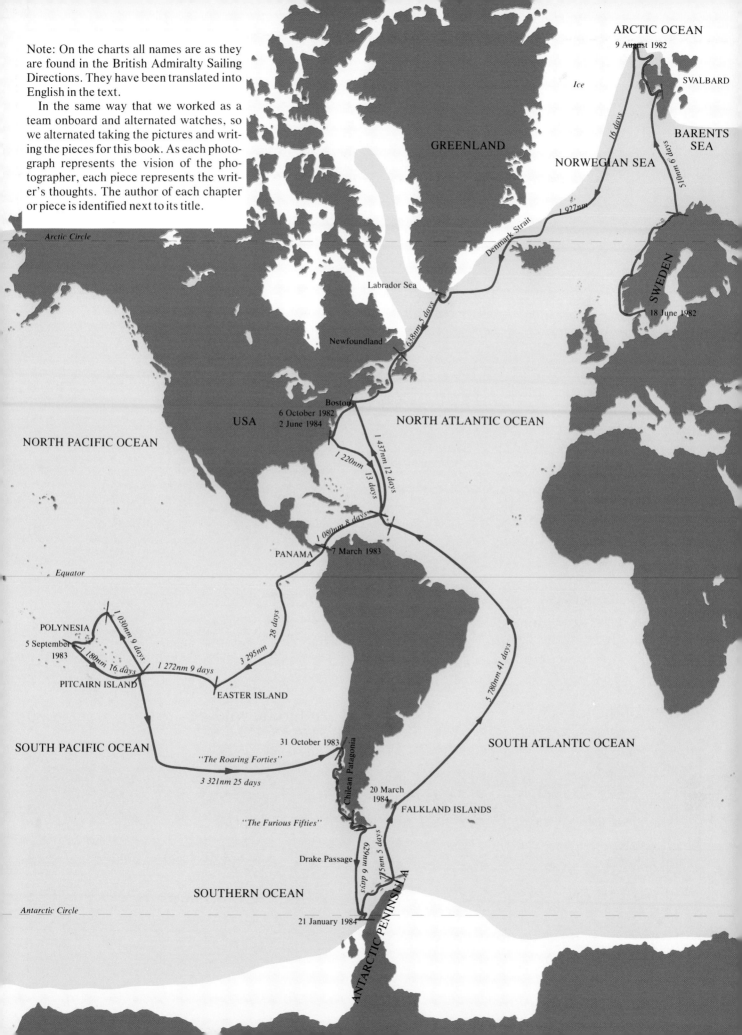

Note: On the charts all names are as they are found in the British Admiralty Sailing Directions. They have been translated into English in the text.

In the same way that we worked as a team onboard and alternated watches, so we alternated taking the pictures and writing the pieces for this book. As each photograph represents the vision of the photographer, each piece represents the writer's thoughts. The author of each chapter or piece is identified next to its title.

ARCTIC OCEAN
9 August 1982

Ice

SVALBARD

NORWEGIAN SEA

BARENTS SEA

GREENLAND

16 days

510nm 9 days

SWEDEN

Denmark Strait

1 927nm

Arctic Circle

Labrador Sea

18 June 1982

638nm 5 days

Newfoundland

Boston
6 October 1982
2 June 1984

USA

NORTH ATLANTIC OCEAN

NORTH PACIFIC OCEAN

1 437nm 12 days

1 220nm
13 days

1 080nm 8 days

PANAMA   7 March 1983

Equator

POLYNESIA
5 September 1983

1 030nm 9 days

180nm 16 days

1 272nm 9 days

EASTER ISLAND

3 295nm

28 days

5 780nm 41 days

PITCAIRN ISLAND

SOUTH PACIFIC OCEAN

SOUTH ATLANTIC OCEAN

"The Roaring Forties"

31 October 1983

Chilean Patagonia

3 321nm 25 days

20 March 1984

FALKLAND ISLANDS

"The Furious Fifties"

Drake Passage

629nm 6 days

775nm 5 days

SOUTHERN OCEAN

ANTARCTIC PENINSULA

Antarctic Circle

21 January 1984

Introduction

A tropical South Pacific island seems an unlikely if not inauspicious locale to begin a polar adventure. Sailing to the ice was certainly the last thing on my mind that muggy morning when I spied a new boat in the anchorage. Red boats are hard to miss; *Northern Light* was no exception. What did make her exceptional was that she was the only boat of our entire group to have entered the Pacific via Cape Horn.

The Horn had only recently recaptured my attention. While cook aboard a square-rigger, in my off hours I had devoured the skipper's library. The stories of a past sailing era meandered in my brain challenging my old opinion that rounding Cape Horn is for fools and madmen only. But the storytellers couldn't come off the printed page; they were mute to my questions. It all remained in fantasy's realm until the red boat appeared.

I rowed over and knocked. Introductions. Onboard. I posed questions, to which I got answers and a living story. Into the conversation I added my dream: a circumnavigation as close to north-to-south as is possible on a sailing vessel. Rolf countered with his future plan: back to Chilean Patagonia and on to the sub-Antarctic islands.

We were in the same current but sailed in opposite directions. I was on my way home; Rolf on his way west, points as yet undeclared. Nothing was even hypothetical at this point, let alone planned. Cryptically I penned into *Northern Light*'s guestbook: We have a date with destiny. Love stories and high adventure have begun on less auspicious ground, seems to me.

(Deborah)

Since I was a young boy, sailing and spending time in the wilderness have been my greatest interests. At first I sailed canoes on Swedish lakes and along the coast of the Baltic Sea. In 1967 I began ocean racing. In 1970 I crossed the Atlantic Ocean in my 7.5-meter midget ocean cruiser. Since 1977 *Northern Light* has been both my home and the platform for my life.

Sailing on other boats prior to commissioning *Northern Light,* I developed a philosophy that would eventually steer the way I outfitted my boat and chose my crew. I came to believe that the level of safety and enjoyment onboard is in direct proportion to the sense and sensors of the crew. I saw that, while modern instruments increased access to information, in their wake they left "technology hangover." I came to prefer sailing with minimum gear and electronics, and to develop human potential and skills.

At sea a human's true being is bared. The naked truth can be either a happy surprise or a nightmarish discovery—both for the person in question and for the rest of the crew. Because as skipper I am responsible for the quality of life on-

2 Deborah Shapiro, born in 1951 in the United States, has sailed farther north-to-south than any other woman. In 1984 she and Rolf together received "The Blue Water Medal of The Cruising Club of America" for their 33,000-mile Arctic/Antarctic voyage.

3 Rolf Bjelke, born in 1936 in Sweden, has skippered *Northern Light* in all oceans and to all continents. He was awarded "The Ship's Bell" by the Swedish Cruising Club for the planning and execution of this polar voyage.

board, I take pains to find crew with emotional strength, who spontaneously exhibit kindness to others, who respect another's way of thinking, who freely show their feelings. Least of all I care if they can sail. To learn boat handling is easy; to learn how to live on a small boat is not easy.

When Deborah joined me in Sweden at the finish of my circumnavigation, we meshed our ideas into a sailing voyage we named: North Ice–South Ice. We planned to sail north from Sweden, as close to the North Pole as possible, then south to the Antarctic Circle, and back. It would take two years, during which time we would cover 33,000 miles and traverse all the earth's climate zones. If successful, *Northern Light* would be the first Scandinavian yacht to reach Antarctica.

There are risks and dangers on such a voyage. The navi-gational difficulties that we will face in the areas the Admiralty Pilot Book calls "outside the usual routes of ships" are: sea ice and icebergs (especially dangerous in poor visibility), freak waves, inaccurate charts, absence of navigational aids, inaccurate compass readings in very high latitudes, and in Antarctica, sudden, violent and unpredictable changes in the weather. Furthermore, a crew of two faces the risk of mental and/or physical exhaustion. Managing the risks one at a time, or juggling more than one will be our testing ground–for survival perhaps. Its successful completion will be a source of exhilaration previously unmatched in our lives. For Deborah and me, this voyage is our way of beginning our lives together. We have everything to gain and everything to lose.

(Rolf)

4 *Northern Light*

1
Aweigh!

(Deborah)

5 *Along the Norwegian coast*

We simply cannot prepare an hour longer. Even though the work lists are not completed, we cast off the mooring lines. *Northern Light,* looking like a freshly dipped candy apple, is underway. She's sailing away from her Swedish home waters and nudging the first zero from her log on a 33,000-mile journey that will bring her—and us—to the icy ends of the earth.

Our shipyard friends, misty-eyed, wave and wave. Fisherman look up from their netting as we pass. We note the slight disapproving shake of their heads, yet both of us smile and wave in response to their choruses of "good fortune."

Two-and-a-half months of dogged preparation preceded this moment. Rolf and I worked maniacally, seven days a week, at least twelve hours a day, doing every job we had the skill and tools to do. We farmed out as little work as possible; it was critical for us to know the boat before leaving for remote parts of the world.

Since I had never sailed onboard *Northern Light,* the preparation time was my opportunity to become intimately familiar with every nook and cranny and all the systems and gear; it was hands-on training. For Rolf, who had bought the bare hull eight years earlier and finished her himself, the work meant critical appraisal and reconditioning of the boat for an arduous voyage. Neither would stop until we had complete trust in the integrity of the vessel.

We began by dismantling the entire boat and rig, searching for any wear and tear from Rolf's recent 65,000-mile circumnavigation. To bring the boat back into prime condition required repairs, replacements, refinishing, rewiring and servicing. Structural changes Rolf designed specifically for this voyage were also made. Included was the addition of an ice-breaker bow, a wedge-shaped piece of steel, welded to the hull to protect the bobstay, a part of the rigging that is especially vulnerable to impact. Then, we provisioned and bought all our charts, reference books, spare parts and materials for repairs. Finally, we dressed the interior in the finest we could afford and revarnished the teak, believing that beauty would be a source of pleasure when the going got rough.

As hard as we worked, we still fell behind. Our energy dwindled each day we remained past our scheduled departure date—and so did our pleasure cruise in Norway—but we kept working. Every minute of preparation was a precious ounce of prevention. Finally Rolf declared: "What we need now, to heal our spirits, reward our hard work and renew our energy, is to take off. We can finish our projects underway." The boldness implied in the word "underway" had magic in it. There was no discussion. No more than an electric, affirming look passed between us before we were casting off the lines.

Our well-wishers and Sweden's granite coastline slip away and the low, sandy hook of Denmark's northern tip appears ahead. The picturesque town there is the home port of a huge fishing fleet, all painted the same pastel blue. We soak up new sights, sounds and a few Danish pastries and then get back to work, oblivious to the midsummer's eve celebrations going on around us.

Leaving Denmark, the working realities of the voyage hit me hard. It is night, and suddenly I am standing my first four-hour solo watch, on a boat that I don't know how to sail. Although I have been crew on many traditional sailing ships, I have always had watchmates and a watch captain; I have never singlehanded a sailboat. Neither have I ever sailed a vessel as small as *Northern Light,* nor have I ever used all the newfangled, modern equipment. I feel gut-wrenchingly alone. My stomach churns.

The realization that I am going to have to catch on to everything before I cause a disaster aggravates my case of nerves. That and the choppy sea conditions make me seasick. And ahead is a fleet of fifty-two course-changing fishing boats... I vow aloud that I will never look romantically at lights on the water again.

5 I had never sailed on *Northern Light* before leaving on this voyage to the north and south ice. With the beauty of Norway surrounding me, I hone my boat-handling skills.

6 *Northern Light* sails in the light of the midnight sun, south of Tromsø.

Minutes stretch painfully; I stare up at the wind indicator atop the mast until my neck and jaw nearly lock. Continually analyzing the situation, I plan for each of many alternate courses of action, settling on none. Somehow we meander through.

I know Rolf needs his rest, and to my relief, I don't have to wake him from his light sleep when things change— *Northern Light* does. Each one of her noises has a specific voice that tells him exactly what is out of kilter, and he often calls to me from the seaberth to tell me what needs to be done.

But I must gather my gumption and actually do things on my own. I'm getting used to the windsteering controls, and I begin trimming the sails in small increments and analyzing the results. Does it make a positive or negative difference? I'm so tense; there is too much I don't know and so much to co-ordinate. It's a bad dream in which I'm an untrained, tone-deaf person trying to conduct a symphony. I would rather do nothing than make a mistake... nonetheless, I continue to push myself to do... do it now... and begin to get the hang of sailing *Northern Light*. Most importantly, I remain active in the face of tension and anxiety, refusing to be intimidated. Withdrawal is not appropriate; sailing is an active endeavor.

After six days of this special anxiety, landfall is a distinct relief for me. Now, we can be up together, exploring Norway's staggering beauty for as long as we like in the twenty-four-hour daylight.

It is a glorious training time for me. I take charge of the boat and course and yet have my captain available when I have a question or need advice. Meanwhile, Rolf continues to finish project after project. By the time we leave Norway, I have become a competent coastal navigator and a better sailor, Rolf has no more lists, and *Northern Light* is ready to face any kind of weather. The preparation for the north ice is complete.

Sadly, we are forced to make our Norwegian inland-waterway passage faster than originally planned. But once we set the route for the trip, the weather and ice conditions set the time line. And we have a date with the North Pole ice cap in mid-August. To get there in time we must press northward.

6 *Twenty miles to Tromsø*

7 Norway's scenery defies even the most majestic description. And the summer has a special magic: the suspension of night-time, when navigational lights are shut off for the season.

7 *Pytteggja peaks in early morning light*

8 Around this point is the beginning of Geiranger Fjord. Its precipitous walls form the backdrop for 3,000-foot waterfalls, which gush after it rains and then slowly dwindle to a mist as fine as a bridal veil.

9 Wide waterways north of Lofoten.

10 Fog continually swirls around the rocky, wind-swept islands of Lofoten, in northern Norway.

Norway's grandeur

Norway's coastline is so convoluted that the 1,650 miles it covers on a north-south line actually contains close to 12,000 miles for us to cruise and peruse. Although we have to skip the wide and shallow southern fjords this time, as well as 150,000 offshore islands, the scale of what we do see is arresting.

The first view of the snow-capped coastal mountains leaves us agog. But before we can explore Norway—or any new country—we must clear the boat through customs and the crew through immigration. After this official contact, we always head for the next and most important stop: the ice-cream parlor.

Then, we are off, to sail the interconnecting and branching waterways to the dead end of the Geiranger Fjord. It, similar to the other west-coast fjords, is narrow, deep and precipitous. The height is unfathomable without perspective. Only the manmade structures give us an inkling... they appear to be built on a doll's scale. We and our little boat are dwarfed.

In the west-coast fjords we find that the weather patterns vary only in degrees of pleasantness; then there is a dramatic change in the area near Lofoten and the maelstrom. It is enshrouded in rain and fog.

To the navigator's delight, Norwegians' respect and concern for seafarers are evident everywhere. The aids to navigation are numerous, are located where the charts say they are, and are in good repair. The bright-orange cone tops on the markers are highly visible. Tie-up eyebolts are sunk into the rocks where it is too deep to anchor. Also, weather forecasts are frequent, reliable, and cover the considerable area north to Svalbard and west to Greenland.

We find humility and openness in the people who live on the coast. Deed defines life here for those who toil to carve a niche from the mountains or the sea. A retired sea captain extends his expertise to us and helps adjust our compass. A college student takes us for a Sunday drive and visits us again a week later. In the north, a shy fisherman slings part of his day's catch into our cockpit and continues on his way home.

Our stay is too short. We will return.

8 *Geiranger Fjord*

9 *Vågs Fjord*

10 *Veröy*

2
Decreasing temperature, increasing confidence

(Rolf)

11 *En route to Svalbard*

Deborah is strapped into the seaberth. She won't get any rest. *Northern Light* is rolling violently, dipping one rail then the other under water, totally becalmed 30 miles southwest of Bear Island.

After a period of heavy pendulating, the motion stops just long enough for me to think that the sea has started to moderate and that soon it will be possible to live a decent life onboard. But the boat isn't still more than ten seconds before everything starts all over again.

Bored and strained from holding on for six hours, we inflate our little rubber dinghy and row away from *Northern Light*. The small boat reacts to the rhythm of the waves very differently from its mother ship. It rises and falls so gently and pleasingly that it is like resting on a cloud.

Once we get far enough away to no longer hear and be bothered by the clanking noise of the halyards banging the masts, our tight-lipped expressions melt away and are replaced by calm smiles.

The storm petrels sitting peacefully on the swells gave me the inspiration for our rowing tour. They are also waiting for the wind, and when it returns they will soar over the top of the waves without as much as moving their wings. Until then the petrels don't waste energy.

Deborah and I speak about the past and next phases of our voyage. We expended a lot of necessary energy both on making *Northern Light* shipshape for this voyage and on Deborah's training. Now as we sail north into Arctic waters, we will have to react to forces in nature that we have never before experienced. We are prepared to try and are excited at the prospect, yet the changes and novelties will be draining. We conclude that rigidity—an inability to adjust to the surroundings—would cause our greatest energy loss. We take the petrels' clue: we will adjust.

The fog is lowering, and we row back to *Northern Light* before she is lost from sight. The poor visibility makes us focus on the ice risk in front of us. Deborah reads aloud from the Pilot Book: a westerly current around South Cape, Spitsbergen, carries ice with it from Barents Sea, and in some years there can be strips of ice along the west coast of Spitsbergen. She looks up at me and asks if I want to wager which we will see first: ice or land. I bet that we will see ice; Deborah bets land.

The wind returns, and we set sail in a moisture-laden fog. It closes out the twenty-four-hour polar daylight, so much so that we feel as though we are cruising in a long gray twilight.

Nearing land in the fog, we grow excited, almost giddy. It will be a challenging landfall; many of our normal aids are useless. The compasses, because of our proximity to the magnetic North Pole, have large, unpredictable deviation errors. And we can't trust the many contradictory lines of position the radio beacons have given us. We can only trust one mechanical navigation aid, namely the depthsounder, and our own constantly exercised senses.

If our position wasn't so uncertain, we would probably muse more on the fact that where we are sailing now was covered by a 300-foot-thick ice cap 10,000 years ago. But for the moment our historical review doesn't extend farther back in time than to the date of the seachart survey, for we are seeking to ascertain our position by matching our depthsounder readings to the marked depths on the chart.

The water becomes turbid rapidly, assuming a yellowish color. We make a few 90-degree turns; the charted depths on our assumed line of position continue to match the readings. Everything indicates that we are up on the Ice Fjord bank and soon can expect to see Cape Linné abeam to star-

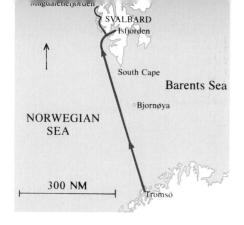

11 *Northern Light* is designed for sailing; when becalmed, the sails no longer stabilize the boat's motion. When the swell is high and the boat rolls, the sails flop, suffering more from strain and chafe than in storm conditions. To avoid unnecessary wear and tear, we drop them and wait for wind.

12 About 60 percent of Spitsbergen is blanketed by glaciers, some that move seaward at a speed of 1–3 yards a day. The dirt swath in the middle of the glacier is composed of sand and rocks that the glacier has worn away from the mountain peaks many miles away from the place where it eventually dumps its cargo into the ocean.

board. Deborah and I take turns reading the depthsounder, and freezing on deck while staring into the fog.

Suddenly we spot a bright light dead ahead. It starts as a tiny patch in the fog. Before we really understand what is happening, the light intensifies so that for a few seconds we are blinded.

When our eyes adjust, we see to starboard rolling hills shifting in shades of green. Dead ahead is an Alp-like landscape with pinnacles and towers of ice. And farther on in Ice Fjord, Nordenskjold Glacier's snowfield glimmers in sunshine. Astern, the fogbank remains a dark impenetrable wall.

The change came so rapidly that we stand speechless until Deborah informs me that she has won our bet: we saw land first, she points out with a great smile. Her eyes flash mischievously as she reveals that she had studied the Arctic Pilot Book carefully during her watches long before we made the bet, especially the section entitled "Frequency of Fog." There might be ice around, but banking on the high fog percentages, she figured we wouldn't see it.

Reviewing the weather statistics, thinking upon bad visibility in combination with ice, Deborah used her intelligence and humor to turn her back on fear; she would not freeze into inactivity. Deborah wins the bet, but I collect the reward: a confirmation of my belief in her ability and strength.

12 *King's Fjord, Spitsbergen*

13 *Ice wall of von Post Glacier*   14 *Blomstrand Glacier*

Ice cycle

At the bottom of Temple Fjord, where the tongue of the von Post Glacier slides into the ocean, we meet ice for the first time on our voyage. From *Northern Light*'s deck we experience one of nature's most powerful spectacles: the birth of an iceberg, a part of a cycle that has been going on for thousands of years. As the ice breaks away, thunderous roars and sharp bangs that sound like gunshots echo between the ice wall and the steep hillsides that frame the fjord.

We keep a respectful distance. Even so, when the glacier "calves" part of its 100-foot-high ice wall, it feels as though we are in the center of the event. When an ice block twice as high as our mainmast topples, its gigantic dimension makes it seem to fall in slow motion, right on top of us. For a moment it looks as though we have gone too close. As the immense peak falls, it drags quantities of smaller ice pieces with it, and the huge mass hits the water's surface with a boom that shakes the rigging.

Half a minute later—or maybe it is a full minute—the resulting swell reaches us. It isn't breaking any longer and only lifts the boat up a few feet. In that moment we spot the ice giant again. It had hit the surface, sunk, disappeared and now reappears halfway between us and the ice wall. With a

hissing sound it rises nearly out of the sea as if shot from an underwater catapult. Then it falls back with a big splash and lies still with only a fraction of its size visible.

Long ago, water molecules evaporated from the ocean and condensed, falling as precipitation over Spitsbergen, making layers of snow which, through their collective weight, compacted into ice and flowed down the mountains to be eventually—today—reunited with the ocean.

13 Huge rivers running under the glaciers carve tunnels big enough for a yacht to sail into.

14 Not every glacier is advancing. Blomstrand Glacier's 100-foot-high ice wall is inactive, which allows us to sail close in front of it.

Note: Of all the ice that is released from the glaciers on the west coast of Spitsbergen, only a very few chunks are big enough to be called icebergs: those that rise more than 15 feet above the surface of the water. That doesn't mean that ice pieces that are visible only a few feet above the surface are of no danger to a sailing yacht. In fact the opposite is true; in heavy sea and/or poor visibility the small pieces are the most difficult to spot. A collision with a bergy bit can be as calamitous as running aground. The result is the same as sailing straight onto a rock: besides the likelihood of ripping a hole in the bottom, the impact will strain the rigging.

18

15 The ice discharged from the glaciers moves forth and back in the fjords with the tide, turning many potential anchorages into temporary stopping places. An ice piece whose visible part is as big as *Northern Light* weighs approximately 250 tons. If it tangles with us, it could very easily make the boat drag anchor or, even worse, break the anchor chain.

16 Bear Harbor is one of the best natural harbors in Spitsbergen and an ideal anchorage. The moraine, left behind by a receding glacier, has been shaped by tidal and wave action into a nook that provides full protection from ice and sea. Additionally, the entrance is too shallow for any big ice pieces to work their way in.

17 Nearly every fjord has its own weather. When we were anchored in New Ålesund and were forced to leave rapidly because of a northwesterly gale, we only had to move 3 miles to Blomstrand Harbor to find sunshine and calm.

15 *Anchored in New Ålesund*

At anchor

In Bear Harbor we haven't any ice worries. Since the boat doesn't need to be looked after and is securely anchored, we make a feast. We can eat and talk as long as we want, and are enjoying being together. As usual, Deborah is in a sparkling mood, so I don't hesitate to ask if she has been upset with me.

She looks surprised, so I explain why I ask the question. Earlier today, when we were in the vicinity of the calving glacier, I asked her to take some pictures of the glacier wall from the rubber dinghy, with *Northern Light* in the foreground. Without the boat as a reference point in the picture, it is impossible to appreciate fully the size of the ice wall.

16 *Bear Harbor and von Post Glacier in Temple Fjord*

17 *Blomstrand Harbor*

18 *Fragile polar life*

Because we are both photographers, I thought that she would feel honored to take the picture. But instead she snapped, "If you want the picture, you can take it yourself." Her voice was irritated in a way which I had never heard before.

Before I even had time to arrange myself properly in the rubber dinghy, she gave the engine full throttle and disappeared with *Northern Light* toward the ice wall. The atmosphere was very tense, and it put me in a bad mood. I took her anger as a criticism of my decision to row around in the little rubber dinghy amidst the ice.

When we finished, she came back to pick me up and was very calm. I hadn't more than put my foot on deck before she—shining like the sun—asked me if I got any good shots.

Already then I started to believe that the earlier Deborah hadn't been as angry as she had looked. Her burst of fury was a mask.

During dinner Deborah explains how she perceives what happened. She wanted as much as I to take the picture, but she was frightened. Not wanting to feel fear, or to show it, fear's cousin, anger, took over.

Anger dominates fear; it makes us strong in the face of anxiety. What I saw reflected from Deborah as anger was the visible result of the battle that she had raging inside herself to muster energy. Had I asked her once more to take the picture, she probably would have jumped in the dinghy and accomplished the task.

The appearance of anger can be a call for help.

19 *Magdalena Fjord*

In the light of the midnight sun

When we drop the anchor late in the evening the boat lies in the shade, but high on the hillsides of Magdalena Fjord the sun colors the snowfields a warm pink. We can't resist the temptation to climb into the midnight sun's magical light.

We are surprised at the ease with which we move upward against the steep and snow-covered hillsides. The fact that we haven't slept for more than forty hours doesn't seem to phase us. The rarefied air and the goal we dream of attaining, to see the midnight sun at exactly midnight, makes us feel not the slightest bit tired.

Deborah and I are playing and chattering. A love-squeezed snowball ends up in my face, but what does it matter? Everything is just for fun, and soon the rays of the sun will dry and warm my face.

It looks easiest to follow the eastern side of the glacier; I walk ahead, breaking trail, and Deborah follows in my footsteps. Soon we are up to the top. Suddenly I hear a scream. When I turn around, I can only see the upper part of Deborah's body and how she maintains her position: arms rigidly stretched and body braced, feet against one side, rear end to the other. Carefully, I retrace my steps and come as close as I dare; I also risk falling through the snow bridge that covers the crevasse.

When I have helped pull Deborah back to safety, we throw a large rock into the hole. For each second that passes our faces pale another shade. When the stone finally hits bottom some seconds later, we feel the fear spreading to the ends of every limb in our bodies.

We realize that what we are doing isn't sane. With my mountaineering experience I should and do know where the hidden dangers are on a glacier. But lack of sleep made me punchy. It drugged me and warped my judgment. I never looked objectively at myself and our decision to take a capricious — and nearly disastrous — walk in the sun.

On our way back to the boat we discuss how to prevent physical and mental exhaustion, for they are without a doubt our biggest threats. Especially since there are just two of us, we have to be very disciplined and satisfy our need for sleep, even when the going is good. Deborah mints the phrase: putting hours in the bank. Whenever possible we have to put hours into our account. We will draw from it to buy safety and therefore life. In the future, because of events that are beyond our control, the account will probably empty both faster and more totally than we would like. But never will a deficit like today's occur again.

We must be able to look objectively at the other's con-

19 Looking down on *Northern Light* while we seek the midnight sun.

20 Out at sea we have seen the sun in the late evening and early in the morning, but it has always been overcast at midnight. Because of the land effect, a clear night is created over Spitsbergen, and even though there are low fog clouds lying over the ocean, we are finally treated to a view of the midnight sun.

21, 22, 23 and 24 (following pages) Polar light conditions are the eye's delight. To a pen-and-ink drawing add a shaft of sunlight. To full sunshine add a stripe of shadow or reflection.

dition. It is very important to openly show our feelings—exhaustion, dissatisfaction, fear, as much as happiness. Yes, we even have the right to be grumpy without having to worry about unfair or challenging criticism from our counterpart. Mood should not necessarily be taken personally by the other teammate. Truth met by fairness and under-standing is the platform on which the voyage rests. We are creating confidence.

When we return to the boat, we see what happened as a useful lesson. Our trek into the midnight sun illuminated issues that will remain brightly lit.

20 *Midnight sun over Reusch Peninsula*

22 *Heading north along Hoel Peninsula*

23 *Magdalena Glacier in midnight sun*

24 *Kvadehuken in early morning light*

3
Assault on the north
(Deborah)

25 *At the edge of the North Pole pack ice with Svalbard astern*

We have hit the wall. Just 3 miles north of the 80th parallel at 13°11′ East longitude and 597 miles from the North Pole, our progress is stopped. All we can see, in an arc that spreads from the northwest to the southeast, are low flat pieces of pack ice. Rolf climbs the mast to survey the situation and thinks he spots Moffen Island less than 10 miles off.

Earlier today Rolf had blown the horn to celebrate the crossing of 80—one goal down. I knew then that I should not expect too much; the edge of the ice is the sailing limit. Now that we are there, goal two is in sight. But Moffen, summer home of the walrus, may as well be a hundred miles away. There is no way for us to reach it; we cannot penetrate the pack ice. This is as far north as we can sail.

The Arctic Ocean freezes solid in the winter. In spring the ice cap begins to recede north and break up. Unfortunately for our hope of getting farther north, two weather factors are against us this year. The spring thaw began early, so the cap is quite broken. And the wind, which affects the ice's movement, has been predominantly out of the

northeast, pushing all the ice south toward the coastline of Svalbard.

We had been waiting for a break in the northeasterly wind, and earlier today it came. We left Spitsbergen in a total calm and entered an ocean trapped between land and ice. An odd feeling crept over us. There was no hint of swell; rocks no more than a few feet above the surface were completely dry. The Arctic Ocean was costumed as a millpond.

After crossing the 80th parallel, we waited for adventure to pounce. She would decide if we could reach Moffen. Most likely, ice would block our path. However, if the barrier was not wide, we could pick our way through in the calm. Or if the calm broke, perhaps the new wind would be southerly and push the ice north...

Naturally, as we talked about calm and southerly wind, the air started to brush our faces—damnably from the northeast. To venture into the pack, with the wind picking up, we risk crushing *Northern Light* between grinding floes or getting trapped for the winter. This is the end of the line.

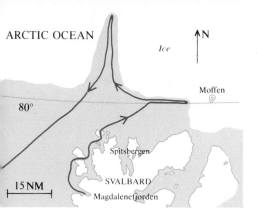

ARCTIC OCEAN

Ice

N

Moffen

80°

15 NM

Spitsbergen

SVALBARD

Magdalenefjorden

25 With Svalbard astern, *Northern Light* sails to the edge of the North Pole ice cap, just north of 80° North latitude.

26 From the top of the mast Rolf sees the outer edge of the pack that continues for 600 miles to the Pole. We dare not enter the maze, since the wind could capriciously close the pathway out.

27 The underwater edge of ice is clearly delineated.

28 I fulfil my promise to bring home the ice.

I am sorely disappointed that we cannot reach Moffen. Aside from a chance sighting, it is the only place we can see walrus. Trying desperately to change my outlook, I force myself to think that the northeasterly wind is good for something... it's a fair wind to sail on now that we must turn toward our next landfall, Greenland. Rolf takes the watch, and I take my tears below and climb into the seaberth to sleep off my frustration. Before I can rest, I have to come to terms with myself. I have forgotten an important maxim of our voyage: have no immutable expectations.

Some hours later, Rolf wakes me for my watch. In the navigation station, while climbing into my foul-weather gear, I glance at the compasses. That they point north is no surprise. Our proximity to the magnetic pole makes them haywire, and I ignore them. If it is not foggy when I get out on deck, I'll take a bearing to land. Spitsbergen should still be in view for some hours.

While climbing out, I am puzzled to see that land is astern, and we are in free water. Rolf tries to keep a straight face, but a sly, telltale smile tugs at his mouth. "I was following the ice's edge west, when a large bay opened to the north. I turned in to investigate and have made five miles. The gap is still wide, and it's all yours."

I take over and hope that the channel will not close behind us, trapping us in the pack. From information on currents in the Pilot Book, I surmise that our bay has been created by the most northerly offshoot of the Gulf Stream. This warm current, transporting heat through the North Atlantic, generally submerges beneath the ice-bearing Arctic Ocean around 80° North because of its higher salinity. What Rolf has discovered is a bit of tropical sass that has refused to sink.

Awake, yet in my ultimate dream—northward still. Feelings of elation grow and the excitement mounts as I steer *Northern Light* just slightly west of north. After a few hours, I see the unmistakable barrier of white ahead and call below to wake Rolf. We're there. It's white on three sides. Time to get the ice.

Rolf takes the helm while I go forward with an axe and bucket and begin to hack away at a piece of ice to fulfil a promise to friends: that one day we will toast the northernmost point with the ice. It's North Pole pack ice from 80°24.7' North at 11°57' East. Its crackling sound in our glasses will remind me of the experiences I will never be able to share fully with anyone but Rolf... of other-worldly places far outside the realm of the familiar... of the range of emotions they elicited... and of all that I learned.

26 *"5/10 pack ice"*

27 *We can't go farther*

28 *80° 24.7' North*

4
Out of the fog

(Rolf)

29 *Ocean-going growler*

29 and 30 The most difficult to spot and therefore the most dangerous of all icebergs are the smallest ones, growlers. Worn smooth, shiny and polished, growlers either tumble like transparent rocks in the water or bob on the surface. As a rule they give no radar echo. For that reason we choose to sail without reliance on radar and develop and trust the most reliable "instrument" of all, our own senses.

30 *Keeping ice watch through cupola*

Fog totally engulfs us. Only when it is possible to see three or perhaps four wave lengths can we keep watch through the cupola inside *Northern Light* and steal a few moments of release from the bitter cold. If the visibility is worse, we stand watch on deck, using the bare skin of our faces to register temperature or humidity changes to alert us to the possible presence of growlers or icebergs.

Our course to Greenland takes us more than 50 miles east of the "maximum limit of icebergs" line marked on the chart. Even still, an unpredictable current could bring ice this far out from Greenland's fjords. And it only takes one iceberg that is not spotted in time to end everything.

For the whole week since we turned the bow south we have been in fog. The ice-watch routine has become robot-

ic: up on the wave crest — search forward, down in the valley — look side-to-side. We look to the sides, not because ice there can harm us, but because it will warn us that there is ice in the neighborhood. Each seven or eight seconds we repeat the monotonous motion: look forward, look to the sides, look forward…

Before going on deck for my watch, I fill the thermos with a hot drink and then try to mete it out to last the entire four hours. If I happen to spill a mugful or if I am freezing and drink everything too fast, I have to do without. For each toe that goes numb in my cold, damp, rubber boots, it takes more and more self-discipline not to leave my post to make something warm to drink. In my chilled emptiness I think: the amount of willpower it takes to carry on stands in direct

N

GREENLAND

SVALBARD

Maximum Limit of Ice

NORWEGIAN SEA

Scoresby Sund

Denmark Strait

ICELAND

NORWAY

300 NM

Chart: On August 10, we leave the North Pole pack ice and head for the southern tip of Greenland. In front of us we have 1,850 miles of variable sailing conditions. The Pilot Book statistics indicate that in the first segment of the voyage we can have 25 percent calm, and until the Denmark Strait 10–20 percent fog. There, the wind charts show 10 percent storm risk and possible hurricane-force winds. At that stage we will have a dangerous combination: dark nights and ice.

31 I check sail trim after an iceberg dictates a course change.

32 Reducing sail because of increasing wind.

proportion to how much one respects one's partner.

On all oceans, even on the heavily trafficked North Atlantic, yachts with more than one crew sail throughout the nights without a lookout. So terrible it must be to be part of a crew where respect for the other peoples' lives is absent. How lonely it is without love.

> Listen little Kittiwake
> Playing in the turbulence of the genoa,
> I have never been happier.
> Let the sail blow up its chest
> And pull with all its might,
> I am as proud
> To safeguard the woman who gives me power.
> Listen little Kittiwake,
> I am freed from my self,
> And can move beyond the horizon of loneliness.

After days of peering out into emptiness it takes many seconds before I really understand that I suddenly am staring at an iceberg of immense proportions. Despite its enormity, I think that the blue shimmering ice mountain is beautiful. But to tell Deborah what I have seen is to give her both a present and a knock-out punch at the same time. So that she will not think that we are in a crisis, I wake her by asking her to come up and bring the camera; I do not tell her what I've seen. She wraps the comforter around herself and pokes her sleepy head up in the cupola. The confirmation that she sees the iceberg that is dead-ahead is a gasp followed by a weak sigh.

After skirting the first iceberg we spot three more and gybe to seek free water closer to Iceland. By dark it is blowing gale- to storm-force wind. We drop all sail in order to drift at the same speed as any icebergs that may be in the vicinity. The sea builds up; heavily breaking waves often slam the starboard side.

Deborah takes the first night watch and sits absolutely still in the cupola, trying to see in the pitch black. I awake suddenly. She is trying to speak, but her voice is obliterated by an ear-numbing crash. I feel the boat being thrown sideways. We have been hit.

In an unsteady voice Deborah says she tried to warn me as soon as she saw the white wall. While it hung suspended over the boat she knew it was the end for us. When the wall smashed into *Northern Light* and dissipated in billions of bright water particles, she understood that it was only a fluorescent wave crest that looked like an iceberg. The rest of her watch she remains busy trying to swallow her heart.

31 *Toward Iceland*

32 *Toward Denmark Strait*

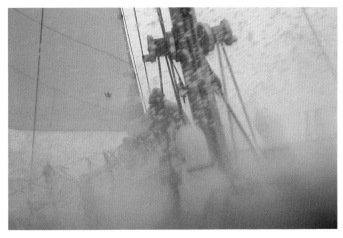

5
Trial by ice

(Deborah)

Icebergs in the fog, hallucinations from the strain, a full gale—all endured with little sleep and less rest—knocked down my resilience. The brain craves rest and peace, but it is not to be. Sailing due south toward Iceland, without a fix for days to verify our position, the coastal radio beacons we have counted on are not working.

It is our opinion that they are being jammed. The morse-code identification signal comes through on-frequency and on-schedule, yet when the directional tone should come on, it turns to garbled noise.

In succession, we try each of the north coast's beacons. None work. The wind is diminishing, but the swell is still high. We continually update our assumed position and monitor the depthsounder to find the edge of the continental shelf. We find it, turn west and round the corner of Iceland into the notorious Denmark Strait.

Taking advantage of the calmer seas, we start the engine to recharge the batteries. After running thirty seconds, the trusty engine sputters and dies. It appears as though, during the gale, salt water has found its way into the tank via the airing pipe on deck.

In the rolling seas, it is not easy to pump the diesel from the one tank to the nearly empty holding tank, and while I clean the emptied tank, the smell makes me nauseous. Now comes the tricky part: doing delicate work with cold fingers in rolling seas to bleed the engine. If anything goes wrong, we will be "powerless" and will soon run out of electricity. Greenland will have to be bypassed, and we will have to head straight for Boston.

Good fortune is with us. Rolf bleeds the salt water from the engine and there is just barely enough juice left in the batteries to turn the engine over and over until it starts.

After all the excitement of the passage from the North Pole pack ice, we are ready for landfall. Seventy miles off the coast of Greenland, the largest island in the world, I think I see the outline of the coastal mountains, backlit by a raging red and orange sunset. Rolf is doubtful, but a check with the binoculars proves me right: the 7,000-foot mountains are unveiled. We lie ahull again for the night because of the ice risk. The wind dies as if on cue; everything is peaceful as we ease into the evening, sharing a relaxed conversation over dinner. I am asleep before my head touches the pillow, dreaming of seas of people and the music their voices make.

What seems like a minute later Rolf shakes me gently. It's time for my watch. Nearing the end of a long passage, the four-hour rotations make an ungodly working schedule, and it's made worse by the lengthening periods of darkness. But

soon, there is a grace of soft morning light above the slick water. I "hoist the iron sail" and get *Northern Light* underway, slowly at first, gently rinsing her veins with what I hope is clean, unwatered diesel. She voices no sputter of dissent.

Rolf takes over the watch. Since it is very cold, we decide to stand two-hour stints at the wheel as we motor toward our destination, the radio station at the mouth of Prince Christian's Sound. Though not particularly tired, I go below and climb into my flannel and comforter cocoon to rest and put some hours in the bank. It will prove to be a wise decision.

The East Greenland fjords are the outlets for the largest single ice cap in the Northern Hemisphere, discharging more icebergs than any other source there. We saw the first piece of ice 50 miles offshore. From information on the Pilot Charts, we had expected it as much as 150 miles earlier. We surmised that the weeks of northeasterly wind had pushed the ice west toward Greenland's coast.

Rolf wakes me later, telling me that he finally sees *the* ice. It's a setup; he has actually been steering carefully around ice for miles. Facing aft, coming out of the hatch, I see thousands of pieces behind us glittering in the bright sunshine. Unfortunately, a clear historical perspective does not prepare me for what I'm about to see ahead.

The impact of the next moment ages me five years; I am stunned. It is not the result Rolf anticipated. He thought he would give me pleasure; he expected me to share his appreciation of the raw beauty of a 10-mile-wide band of enormous icebergs and pack ice in orbit around Greenland. What dazzles Rolf terrifies me.

Looking from the edge into an ice jam, it seems more densely packed than it really is. Hypothesizing that the fjord will have a current flowing out from it, creating free water for us, we continue westward. We pick our way through easily at the beginning.

While marvelling at the shapes and sizes of these behemoths, we name a lot of them. One berg is the spitting image of Charles de Gaulle, another the Houston Astrodome. But the fun evaporates as thunderous cracks signal the disintegration of the Astrodome, and neighboring bergs rock in the resulting swell. Some of them capsize.

The third distinct jam we reach is the end of the line. We can see our destination, but from the top of the mast Rolf realizes that it is impossible for us to make it through the 3-mile-wide ice jam. The pieces are too large for us to push out of the way, and too closely spaced for us to pick a path through.

Time is our concern. We have been working our way in through the ice for more than four hours, and we have to get

GREENLAND

N

Prins Christians Sund

Aappilattoq

LABRADOR
SEA

Kap Farvel

30 NM

33 and 34   Rolf climbs the mast to survey the situation ahead. His view from the mast is of the ice jam that separates us from our destination, the radio station at the mouth of Prince Christian's Sound, in southern Greenland.

33 *Prince Christian's Sound*

34 *Looking for a path*

35 Greenland's ice cap flows from two interior domes to the coast and discharges ice into the fjords. More icebergs come out of Scoresby Sound on Greenland's east coast than out of any other major outlet. They move south in the current around Cape Farewell, and then north along the west coast. Icebergs can last for more than two years, eventually melting away along the coast of Labrador or Newfoundland.

It is not wise to be in a narrow fjord when bergs this size are calved; the resulting swell can start breaking and capsize a small vessel.

out and into free water before dark. Assuming we'll find it around the southern tip, we head out on a southeast course.

The swell increases and the visibility decreases. The large bergs are behind us, but we must contend with growlers. It was easier to spot and steer around them when the sea was flat; now we must pick our path from the crest of each swell. I'd like to slow down, but we have to maintain speed and search for a decent place to lie ahull. As we clear the southern tip of Greenland, the swell and fog disappear, but there are dark, frontal lines in the sky to the south. We may have bad weather, darkness and icebergs tonight.

The sight of ice is becoming oppressive. I just don't want to look at it any longer. As I go below to hide, I offer to make us a cup of hot chocolate. Standing at the stove with portholes before me, I watch the ice sliding by, piece after piece. There is no respite.

Soon we discover an area free of growlers. I breathe a deep sigh of relief. We continue south away from the coast, since the chart cautions that there can be an onshore set of up to 3 knots. It will carry us back toward the coast as we drift through the six hours of darkness.

Over dinner Rolf and I discuss strategy. There are seven gargantuan bergs that will drift toward shore with us during the night. Tomorrow morning we will attempt to enter the interconnecting matrix of fjords from the southwest, assuming that in the lee, the coastline will not be jammed with ice. I offer to take the first night watch.

Before Rolf goes to sleep, we have another look around our neighborhood. Oddly, the bergs' arrangement has changed. We reckon that because of their extreme depth, these large bergs are moving in a different current from the one that is transporting *Northern Light* toward the coast. Our strategy is modified in the light of the new information; we will not drift with the bergs, we will oppose them. The Pilot Book states that bergs have been observed to move as much as 40 miles a day in this vicinity. We will keep a constant lookout and motor out of their way, if necessary.

While dressing for my outside stint, I comfort myself that at least I knew their positions before it got dark. But as I open the hatch minutes later, I freeze... fog has settled in, obliterating any view. I can see my way around on deck, but not as far as the masthead light 50 feet above.

Staring out into the primeval soup it is impossible to ascertain distance. My mind strains for clarity and my eyes to focus. I have to concentrate to look at nothing in particular and take in the whole. I see a slight blur, a smudge on the evenness of the fog... a cloaked iceberg. I have no way of knowing how far away it is. Another berg is close enough to hear. The waves hitting the base sound like breakers on a shoreline; it is abeam and moving past us. The blur, nothing more than a nebulous shadow, is what I have to wait for. My stomach tightens.

I am alone, pinned between fear and icebergs, with both closing in. Old doubts take voice in my mind. How well will you cope with a situation so threatening and so far outside the realm of the familiar? How long until reality is distorted by false perception? How long will creative suppleness remain before it warps into hallucination?

The biggest problem is the waiting itself; there is nothing to work on and nothing decisive to do. The key word is "do." *Do something. Move around. Start your normal exercise routine.* But I am too jittery and feel that I could too easily trip or fall over the side. *So go now and get your safety harness.* The last bastion of logic has split off into the watch partner I so desperately need. It is taking control and keeping me calm.

I go below, get my harness and short tether, return on deck and hook in. Again, my "partner" directs me: *Keep busy.* How? Singing, multiplication tables? *Be serious. Your night vision can't pinpoint. Let your eyes dart around and at different focal lengths. Don't assume a horizon in the fog. Free your peripheral vision. Keep watch 360 degrees.*

The blur moves across the bow, and the fuzz becomes dark patches. They are gradually getting larger, yet it is impossible to ascertain the distance that separates them from us. I know that in the absence of much light one sees dark things better—but why would an iceberg be dark? Perplexed and anxious, I wait. My repertoire of songs runs dry.

An hour elapses, and the patches loom larger. Of course it's a berg, but I can't figure out how long it will be until it rams us. I start to get dizzy—at the end of my rope. But panic is not an option; when the fear gets this intense, I must go for help.

Convinced it's close, I can't spend much time below. Tersely I tell Rolf to wake up. His eyes zing open. I tell him that it's time for us to move out of the way. He should come look for himself... but don't expect white... it's dark patches. I fly back up on deck. Rolf doesn't even dress. He opens the hatch, looks and looks some more and before disappearing tells me to come down when I get a chance. I know he hasn't even seen it.

"Deborah, it will be dangerous if I don't get some sleep. We have no guarantee of landfall tomorrow or in Greenland for that matter. These bergs are not steaming along at six

35 *Only one-ninth of an iceberg is visible*

36 *It is 600 feet deep*

knots. When one comes close, you'll hear it and we'll have plenty of time to move out of its way. If we move now, we'll risk motoring too close to another one you don't see.''

Fear had stymied logic. Blinded by the fog, I had fought to see; I should have been using my ears. I go back up on deck with purpose. But I know Rolf didn't see the patches and probably thinks I am totally irrational. Luckily, that makes me angry. Although anger itself is not appropriate, it displaces the fear, liberating me from the menacing internal inhibitor. And anger can be twisted slightly into a useful tool: the fighting spirit. I am released.

Not long after, a swatch of clear sky and stars appears suddenly. I see that my patches are the huge flat vertical facets of a geometrically shaped iceberg and that they are connected by mammoth arcs of white. Of *Titanic*-sinking proportions, it disappears promptly into its foggy shroud. But now it is a known value.

Minutes later, I hear it. It's getting close. I wake Rolf and tell him that it is time to move. He drags himself out of his bunk again and takes a quick listen. This time he grabs for his clothes and asks me to give some throttle; he'll turn the key.

It takes us fifteen minutes to motor halfway around the base of this berg. The sky begins to clear as Rolf takes over. On his watch he has starshine and a brilliant display of aurora borealis. Hell is a private experience.

37 and 40 *In Prince Christian's Sound, mountains yield to the earth-shaping power of glaciers*

38 and 39 *Around any bend in a fjord, our path may be blocked by ice*

Inside Greenland's fjords

During the night the current transported us northward to within a few miles of Cape Farewell. We set sail at first light, found a channel relatively free of ice, and finally see the color green for the first time since Norway, 3,000 miles and thirty-five days ago. Our senses are flooded with the sights, smells and sounds of land. Motoring through the maze of waterways, gazing at the bold mountains, we find we are still drawn toward Prince Christian's Sound. Perhaps we can reach the radio station from the west, if there is room to maneuver around icebergs.

Along our meandering way, we find a delightful spot near the mouth of a creek. We drop the hook and *Northern Light* rests, swaying gently at anchor. There are only large bergs in sight and we are protected from them by something as simple as shallow water. A peaceful feeling envelops us.

We sleep for a few hours. I come up on deck just after the tide has changed. A flotilla of bergy bits is just about to foul our anchorage. Each is at least the size of the boat and one is heading directly toward our anchor chain.

Rolf and I watch it hit the chain. It is a rare, odd wish that the holding wasn't so good. The chain stretches from the weight of the iceberg. The anchor doesn't budge, the chain has no more slack, something has to give. It is the berg's move, and it begins to rotate, spinning free of the chain.

Time to go. We leave for a small cove marked on the chart as an anchorage with a settlement. The way to it has been shaped by the glaciers, whose profound powers are visible in the chopped and carved landscape.

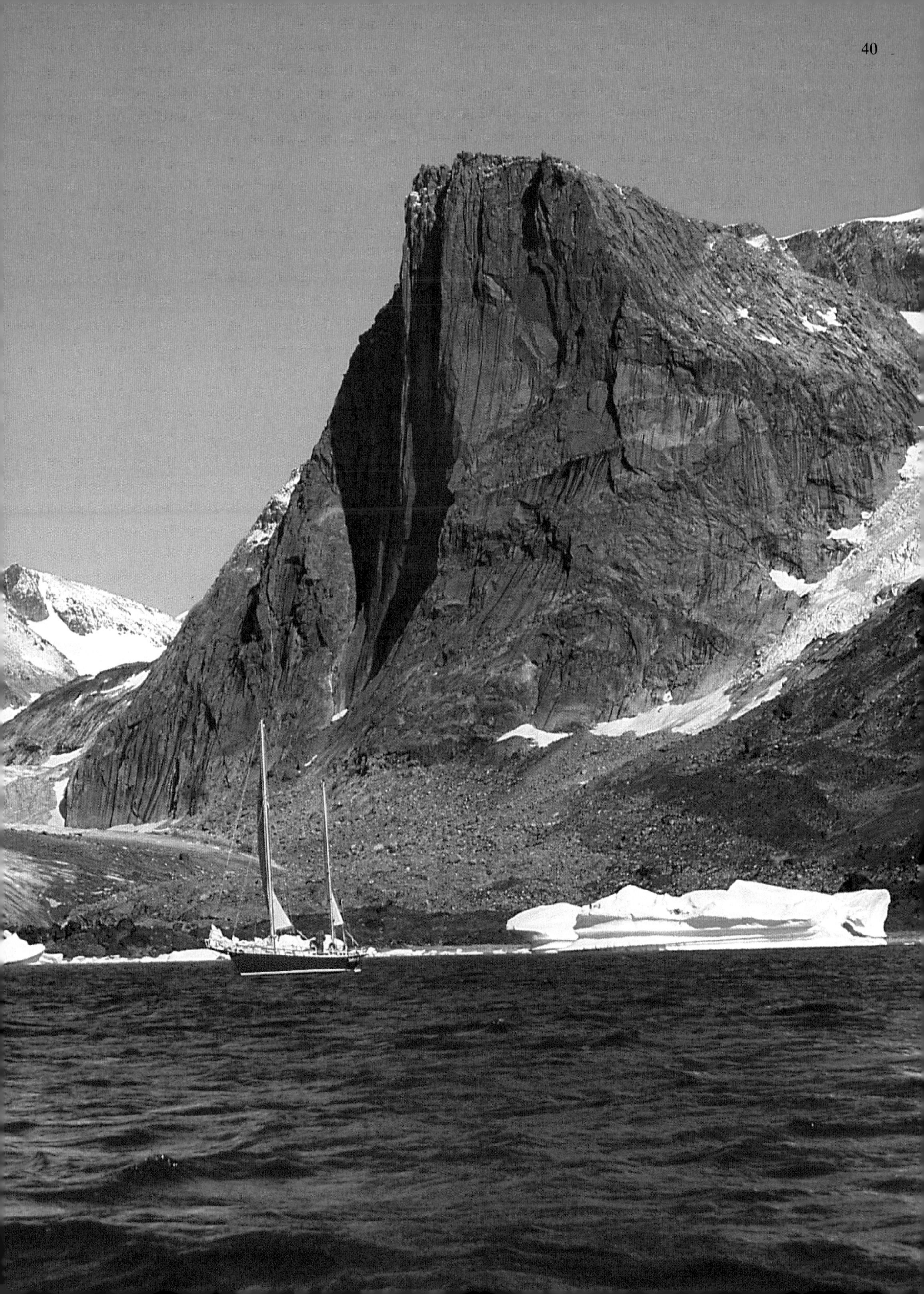

41 *Ice sculpture*

Water, in all its forms, is a powerfully erosive force. Just as a glacier leaves its mark on the land, water leaves its mark on icebergs. Both above and below the waterline, icebergs are constantly worn down by water, continually sculpted in the process.

The surface below water is constantly melting, losing its sharp edges and becoming smooth. The surfaces above water are also in a constant state of change; they melt in the sunshine and are battered by windswept water. Waves and tidal changes leave marks on bergs, scalloping their waterlines. Waves also form and continually enlarge indentations and arches in the ice, often to cavernous proportions. As a berg melts it may become unstable and capsize, exposing the smoothened surface.

Northern Light could have easily fit under the arch, but Rolf did not attempt to sail through it—icebergs give no warning before capsizing. And I did not motor through in the dinghy—noise can fracture them.

42 *Deborah out on photographic foray*

A foam-filled survival suit like the one I'm wearing is "de rigueur" for dinghy trips in water that is around or below 32°F. Salt water freezes at temperatures below fresh water; we will experience water as cold as 28°F. Without the survival suit, our life expectancy in 32°F water is measured in minutes, and with it perhaps hours.

6
In harmony with the weather
(Rolf)

43 *Aappilattoq, Greenland*

When we depart Greenland for Canada we must be in harmony with the following complex weather situation:

– Large temperature differences are most favorable for the development of lows. The most frequent and violent frontal activity in the world occurs around the southern tip of Greenland, where the warm water from the Caribbean meets the very cold air that slides out from the Greenland ice cap.

– We will sail on a major depression track, but in an opposing direction, therefore we must expect to be hit by at least one depression on our passage from Greenland to Canada.

– Of the 600-mile passage the middle 200 miles have lower percentages of fog and iceberg risk.

– From August to September the risk of storm doubles at Cape Farewell, and the risk of fog halves along the Labrador coast.

Our plan is to leave on the tail end of a cold front, hopefully before the first fall storm, to be in the "ice-free middle" of the Labrador Sea when we meet the next depression, and to arrive in Canada in sunshine.

On the last day of August, *Northern Light* lies at the dock in the harbor of an Innuit village; we are waiting for the seasons to change. Just before dark last night the wind shifted against us, and the ice from the fjord began crowding into the bay. By the time we went to bed it was blowing pretty hard and snowing. I felt frozen, but each time the ice squeezed against the topsides and the mooring lines squeaked around the bollards, I had less need of covers. My chest was sticky from perspiration, and I was wracked with anxiety, waiting for daybreak.

Now at first light I can see that the result of the windshift is just as I feared: ice has plugged the harbor. An Innuit up early skinning seals tells me that it's winter now. To give more power to his words he points up to the surrounding mountains that have a dusting of snow. He explains that when the snow stays as it does now, summer is gone.

We are fortunate; yesterday's snowstorm stopped a visiting hospital boat from leaving the harbor. It and a small freighter that was scheduled to leave today now start to apply their combined horsepower to break the ice. At first nothing happens; then slowly the freighter starts to move its weight through the ice. Dangerously close behind follows the doctors' boat. The tactic becomes clear: as soon as the freighter's hull slides away from the ice, the cleared path starts to close. The hospital boat remains close astern to the freighter to keep the channel open. We remain as close as we can in the clear water behind the doctors' boat and have to give full throttle to remain the third bead on the string.

Suddenly the hospital boat dips. It has hit an underwater shelf of a big ice flake. If the boat stops we will ram its stern and break our bowsprit. Fortunately it slides off the shelf and maintains speed. Seconds later, although eons have passed, we are out in free water. I turn to wave goodbye to the friends we made in the village; already there is no sign of the crack where we broke through the ice. In a small tense voice Deborah wonders where we should go.

Last night when I couldn't sleep because of the ice scratching against the topsides, I got up to study the charts and found a shallow bay that is sheltered from the new wind direction. We will sail there and drop the anchor in 7 feet of water. Because icebergs in the fjord have 35- to 600-foot drafts, I am convinced that no ice will disturb this night's sleep. Very proudly I tell Deborah, "Tonight you can sleep peacefully; our last Greenland anchorage will be ice-free." But Deborah is disbelieving. She wants to bet. I accept, happy to have the chance to win my first wager with her.

During the night the rain pours down and we sleep like logs. But in the early morning a strange sound penetrates through the hull, waking us up. Through the skylight I see that the sky is clear. It's cold in the boat so I don't rush out of bed. Instead I try to start a conversation with Deborah. "We'll get going as soon as we can to take advantage of the fact that the cold front has just passed. If we are lucky…"

Deborah doesn't listen to me; she focuses on the strange clicking sound that transfers through the hull. She jumps out of bed, opens the cupola, and looks out. With a hop she's back to me with the information that she has won the

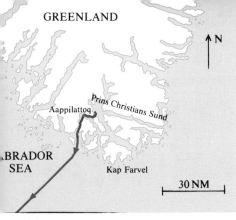

44 *Leaving Greenland*

43 The wind shifts, and every piece of ice that is small enough to fit through the harbor's narrow mouth manages to do so, jamming *Northern Light* against the dock in Aappilattoq Harbor. It is time to leave.

44 Cutting our way through plate ice to depart from Greenland. *Northern Light* was iced in overnight when raindrops froze on the colder salt water.

45 From a single raindrop, freezing plate ice grows in a concentric pattern to form lilypad shapes.

45 *Plate ice*

bet. *Northern Light* is locked in half-an-inch-thick plate ice. We are hearing ice scratch the hull as it moves out with the tide.

When I try to trip the anchor, instead of the windlass handle moving, I slide back and forth on deck. Last night's rain has turned the deck into a skating rink. After I chip away enough ice to get decent footing on the non-skid deck covering, I manage to trip the anchor out of the clay bottom, and we begin to cut our way to freedom. It's the last time I'll wager with Deborah.

7
Between extremes

(Deborah)

46 *Rolf takes a moon sight in the tropics*

During each of the first five nights that we slept in my home in Boston, I walked in my sleep. My mission: to check our anchorage. Each time, I woke Rolf to report imminent peril, most often that we were dragging. What else could explain the proximity of the trees?

The voyage to the north ice had taxed all my limits. More than physically tiring, it was mentally and emotionally draining. We both needed to unwind. So although it was possible to leave immediately, sail directly to Antarctica, and arrive there in summertime, we decided that it was not the prudent route to the south ice. Instead a detour in tropical waters—a relaxing vacation cruise—was designed. The planned route: to the Virgin Islands, through the Panama Canal, to Easter Island, Pitcairn Island and Polynesia. Built in were tactical benefits as well: we would have time to keep *Northern Light* in top shape; we could replenish provisions easily; and we could try to find two more crew members for the tougher southern segment of the voyage. I had a personal plan as well—to leave the rank of novice behind, I planned to learn celestial navigation.

This vacation in the middle changes our life's ambience drastically, but it is hardly a difficult adjustment. With friends along, watches are shortened and time off lengthened. The weather gets warmer; we discard layers of clothing and eventually enjoy standing night watches on deck. The Caribbean nights carry us on our way; the water is mercurial and luminescent, a mirror image of the starry sky.

Out in the South Pacific Ocean, we stand watch, eat fresh fish when we're lucky, gaze at tropical displays of humid pastels at sunset, nestle into the cobalt-blue star-studded dome at night, and are enraptured when the full moon's steely light meshes with daylight's glowing pink somewhere behind a cloud. Then, twenty-nine days out of Panama, a most intriguing spit of land appears ahead.

What remains on Easter Island of a lost civilization keeps us entranced for three weeks. Who carved and erected the looming stone statues here, and what motivated them to do it, remains a mystery. That every statue transported to a place along the perimeter faces the interior of the island fascinates us; in fact, we amateur anthropologists onboard *Northern Light* have a hypothesis.

We figure that the people who came here by sea were already statue builders. When they sighted this island with its high sheer sides, they circumnavigated to look for landing places. As they closed the coast, they passed a high pinnacle-shaped volcanic chunk of rock that sits just offshore. Looking at it from the side as we did, they saw facing in toward the island, the outline of a face—and regarded it as the profile of the spirit or protector of the island.

They landed in a sandy cove on the northern shore and erected a singular statue of their leader. Then they began carving likenesses of this "Great Protector" and moved them to sites all around the perimeter of the island. Like the original, all the copies face the interior, contemplating the two volcano craters, which accounts for the name they chose for their island: Navel of the World. Well, we think it's a plausible theory.

Pitcairn Island, next link on the chain of islands leading us to the south ice, fiercely underlines our belief that living with the sea, in response to nature's systems, is a primary and powerful existence. Surrounded by salt water, not supportive of human life since our phylogenic predecessor forsook its Mother Sea in favor of life ashore, we exist in an erosive and life-threatening environment. It constantly reminds us just how fragile life is and what dedication it takes to carve out a niche for oneself. In this way our lives match the lives of the inhabitants of remote Pitcairn Island, a tiny tip of a volcano that found its way above the surface of the ocean.

Pitcairn is a special place with its own intriguing style evolved in isolation. The fifty people who live here remain for a life that cannot be duplicated elsewhere. Where else but a tiny speck in the middle of the sea could such spirit of cooperation and purity prevail? Where else could a person

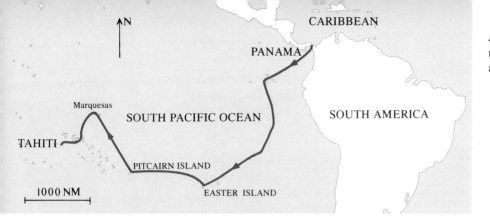

47 For a peaceful pause, we meander through the South Pacific Ocean; the sun and the moon mark the rhythm of our lives.

live by the motto: ''Anyone who is friendly to me is my friend,'' as Andrew Young does? Both Rolf and I would be proud to be counted as a friend by any one inhabitant of this island. Our three weeks here are idyllic, punctuated by near disaster when three of their open boats face a 5-mile return trip in a gale after offloading tons of supplies from a freighter.

Our last fling is in French Polynesia. We visit the Marquesas, Tuamotus and Society Islands, where we swim, snorkel, run, and feast on fresh fruits and vegetables. When all our friends leave for home, we sail back to Tahiti to provision for the next ten months plus an additional six months of emergency supplies, and to comb junkyards and marine hardware stores for the gear, spare parts and materials for repairs for the 17,500 miles ahead of us.

The conditions we experience during the passage from Bora Bora to Tahiti are the worst ever. The wind continually changes direction and intensity, the sea comes from every which way, and the current is ferocious. The boat pounds; rest is impossible. A sail that took us fifteen hours one way takes an agonizing sixty-two hours the other. In Papeete harbor, our anchor chain will not pay out; from being airborne during the pounding, it is tangled in knots!

The news the next day does not come as a surprise. A nuclear device had been tested in the seabed in a remote part of French Polynesia. One minor result was the confused sea; the shock waves had reverberated through the water, bouncing around on the underwater mountains. When will this madness be stopped?

47 *In the South Pacific*

48 *Toward stone statues in Anakena Bay, Easter Island*
49 *Stone statue's silhouette*

50 *Pitcairn Island's dry side*

Risky stops

Fate plays a part in any yacht's visit to Easter and Pitcairn Islands. Neither has a protected harbor for boats with any draft, nor are there safe anchorages. One finds a modicum of protection in the lee, drops the hook and hopes for the best. The major problem is that the swell around these islands does not necessarily come from the prevailing winds, but from the pulse of the depressions in the Roaring Forties. Heavy weather in the south often sends swells—emissaries that arrive without warning since they have nothing to do with the local weather pattern. They break so heavily on the shore that landing becomes impossible.

Worse is to be onshore when the swells appear and begin breaking. Then one is caught there helplessly watching the yacht heaving in the swell, straining her chain, because the dinghy can't get out through surf. Our solution: at least one person stays onboard during the night and as needed during the day. And while onshore, we take turns keeping watch for changes in the sea conditions. Many yachts have been lost at these islands, and indeed most yachts are lost on shorelines, not at sea. Where we drop anchor is nothing more than an open roadstead and the skipper has the gray hairs to prove it. Still, we think they are worth it.

50 St. Paul's Pool on Pitcairn Island is high above sea level, and fills from swells originating in the Roaring Forties.

8
The Roaring Forties

(Rolf)

51 Heavy weather is approaching
Feathery cirrus clouds are the forerunners of depressions, messengers which warn us in the Roaring Forties—the Southern Hemisphere's powerful westwind drift—that our heavy-weather sails should be within easy reach.

Except for the weak light from the kerosene lamp at the navigation desk it is dark inside the boat. Deborah is sitting on the ladder with her head in the cupola, keeping watch in the gale while I try to sleep. The sea is running from the stern quarter, and mostly *Northern Light* sails upright. But from time to time when the boat heels heavily, rivers of water run along the rail and pour out through the scuppers. Above the seaberth one-eighth inch of steel separates me from the water... but not from the gushing noise. It continually wakes me, and each time I come to, I also hear that the wind has intensified. Its din hardly resembles wind any longer. Eventually I can't fall back to sleep. The weather is accelerating toward the next stage. I have the feeling that it will soon be time...

My mind drifts to the face of a friend, Hasse Nilsson, captain of the *Lindblad Explorer,* and to a story he once told me. Once his vessel was hit hard on the side by an enormous wave. A woman passenger standing in the reception area didn't have the strength to hang on during the impact and flew the length of the counter, across the passageway and through a closed door. Hasse was on the bridge at the time. When he heard about the incident, it saddened him—it was a very beautiful and irreplaceable door, he told me.

Deborah calls to me, using my name only. By agreement that brevity means business, and it pierces my consciousness. She tells me that it is time to drop the mainsail. Climbing out of the seaberth, I really hang on; it took Deborah a lot of time to build and varnish the cabinets on the lee side.

Out on deck in the dark the atmosphere is spooky—a world of water and fire. Wave crests look like lit torches that are then instantly extinguished, drowned in the ocean, and yet leave behind fields aflame. As I check the sea conditions, listen to the rigging's song, and decide whether or not it is time to reduce sail, a wave smacks the topsides. Its fluorescent spray lights up the entire main. As the water runs off, the sail looks as though it is melting and disappearing in streams along the boom. With each successive wave I too become luminous, and while I drop the mainsail each carefully placed footstep glows. Looking over the rail into the water, I see the propeller and the entire rudder even more clearly than in daylight. *Northern Light*'s wake is a comet's tail.

The spectacular show continues even while I keep watch inside. Each sea that splashes over the cupola turns it into a planetarium, the dome filled with falling stars. The night's fireworks make me forget totally that it is blowing a full storm. When twilight comes the ocean changes its guise, but its new face is at least as dramatic. Just before the largest seas break, a 60- to 90-foot-long turquoise tunnel appears under the white crest. Seconds later the charge turns on itself, and the crest dissipates in tumbling foam. Those surfaces which were luminescent in the dark now glitter like huge snowfields.

Even though the breaking seas often almost submerge the windsteering vane, *Northern Light* never shows the slightest tendency to be thrown abeam to the sea. Keeping speed, she tracks along the foam streaks that connect one wave to the next.

As if by the wave of a magic wand the entire picture changes when the cold front arrives. The wind becomes so strong that it no longer pushes waves to crest—it instead chops off their tops. Just above the water's surface, the concentration of hurling water droplets is so dense that it sometimes blocks out my view of the sea.

After watching this a while I can't resist waking Deborah. I want her to encounter the excitement of more than 50 knots of wind in the open ocean. After all, it's not often that one has the chance to experience such exhilarating natural forces.

52 *Sunrise in a 50-knot storm*

53 *Storm wave slams the boat and buries the windsteering vane*

54 *This wave moves at 30 knots. Close the hatch quickly before the wave breaks.*

Life onboard

Our watch system is based on a four-hour rotation. To alternate the schedule so that one of us doesn't always have two night watches and the other the dreaded midnight watch, we split an afternoon watch into two two-hour stints, thus changing the rotations each day. In two days my watches are:

1000−1400	10:00 a.m. − 2:00 p.m. (lunch chef)
1600−1800	4:00 p.m. − 6:00 p.m. (dinner chef)
2200−0200	10.00 p.m. − 2:00 a.m.
0600−1000	6:00 a.m. − 10:00 a.m. (breakfast chef)
1400−1600	2:00 p.m. − 4:00 p.m.
1800−2200	6:00 p.m. − 10:00 p.m.
0200−0600	2:00 a.m. − 6:00 a.m. (da capo)

We are both very interested in cooking, or more honestly in eating, and we appreciate not having the same meal served more than twice a month, with the exceptions of Deborah's spaghetti sauce and my cabbage casserole. Even in heavy weather we bake two loaves of bread every second day. As soon as these morsels come out of the oven, one is placed strategically out of reach. Then we plant ourselves cozily on the floorboards in front of the oven with a steaming-hot loaf and a dish of butter between us. Although the thick slices are almost too hot to hold, the butter doesn't melt before the first piece is inhaled. Then we get serious: the second slice gets a glop of marmalade on it. By slice number three, accolades may be heard between the chewing.

The worse the weather the more hot meals we prepare. This principle has both physical and mental rewards. A hot meal not only heats up our bodies and provides energy, it also nourishes our self-respect by having accomplished the task of reaching above the level of mere existence.

For us the word "bunk" creates the sense of a place where one might rest a little if the sleeping bag isn't too wet. We don't have such a place onboard *Northern Light;* in our eyes, the seaberth is a bed. There we sleep between flannel sheets with a fiber-filled comforter covering us. The rest in this cocoon is worth five times as much as the rest we would get in a bunk or dressed in oilskins on the cabin sole.

Heavy-weather seamanship requires quality deckwork engineered by a person with a clear mind and a strong, rested body. The quality of deckwork therefore remains in direct proportion to the quality of life you have below deck; good seamanship starts there.

56 Our seaberth can be canted to compensate for the heeling angle so that we always sleep level. In heavy weather the safety belt keeps us from being thrown out of the bed.

57 With less than 100 watts output from her amateur radio, Deborah is able to reach Boston, USA, for her weekly schedule with Andrew L. Morrison, whose call sign is N1BHI.

59 I update our continuous dead reckoning and celestial line of position. The satellite navigator installed in Tahiti remains moisture-free behind a vinyl cover when not in use.

55 *Ladle boiling water to avoid burn accidents*

58 *Swedish chef in action*

56 *Belted into the seaberth*

57 *Morse code contact with N1BHI*

59 *One hundred and ninety-four miles in 24 hours*

60 *Maintenance work in comfort below deck*

Heavy weather

Each ocean has its own life, its own pulse, and its own disposition for us to learn and understand. Meeting a new ocean is like entering a new culture—you must know the prevailing etiquette; otherwise the penalty can be severe.

There is a distinctive difference between the rules and forces which prevail at sea and the laws and powers which prevail in a human society: the sea knows no evil. The rules of the sea are constant and impartial. Yet men tend to anthropomorphize and turn the sea into a cruel, angry foe. An enemy is created. Such pointless rage consumes energy unnecessarily.

Nature's law for people at sea is simple: he who adjusts survives. In storm conditions we must first accept. We must drop expectations overboard instead of letting them steer, and then we must adapt to the natural forces that are in motion.

Before we left the easy life of the trade-wind belt, Deborah and I discussed how we could best sail safely and save our energy. Her motto, "Do It Now," is a key to staying ahead of problems and changes. We try not to wait until we're forced to do a job even though this often means working when we would rather enjoy ourselves or when we are tired. Inactivity is a great danger. Inactive people do not adjust the boat to changing conditions; inactive people do not gain experience. The more we work on deck, the more certain our footing and actions become, the more easily we make decisions. Then both safety and fun increase.

On every vessel, boat-handling theory sets safety parameters. I believe *Northern Light* should always be sailed as close to her potential speed as possible, because then she fits best to the sea, and her motion is most pleasant. With speed in heavy weather she has momentum. Slamming waves hit her and are shattered; she stays on course.

With deepening insight our time at sea becomes a fascinating interplay between crew, boat and ocean, even in storm conditions. Long-distance cruising is so much more than trimming sails.

Twenty-one days of alternating watches in the Forties, yet neither of us considers resting the night we approach the Chilean coast of South America. At sundown we sail over the continental shelf, and the sea dwindles to nothing. It is a clear indication that the tide is rising, that the stream is with us. We therefore continue as planned toward the Gulf of Coronados, north of Chiloe Island.

At midnight we realize that although we are making

speed, we are no longer moving forward. The wind is with us, all reefs are shook out, and the biggest genoa is set, but slowly and surely the outgoing tide is pushing us toward the open ocean. The current is so strong that although the log shows 7.5 knots speed, we are moving in reverse, up waves that make no speed over ground.

The boat climbs stern-first up the waves, which are about 12 feet high, exceedingly steep and breaking. She hangs on the crests for a couple of seconds, with most of the rudder in the air. At that moment, the breaking wave is level with the lifelines and pours into the cockpit from both sides.

With the rudder airborne, we lose all control. Only when the boat dips aft and slides down into the next valley do we

get steering capability back. When the tide is at its strongest there isn't more than four boatlengths' distance between the breaking seas—every ten seconds *Northern Light* is on the verge of being knocked over. Never has wearing our safety harnesses been more important, not even in a full storm mid-ocean.

At twilight the rip diminishes. There is no slack water here; we start to gain ground immediately. Deborah takes over the helm as we are sucked into Chacao Channel. When we are through she verifies that only a little more than an hour was needed to make 15 miles, while it had taken me eight hours to cover that distance when the tide was against us.

61 *The cold front has passed. Time to reset the mizzen?*

Although *Northern Light* is ketch-rigged, in more than 25 knots downwind we sail her as a sloop. By dropping the mizzen and carrying the biggest headsail possible for the wind strength, we effectively move the center of the sail plan forward. That keeps the boat stable on course, which has meant so far that the wind-steering has been able to keep the boat on course in any heavy-weather condition.

Northern Light is designed for sailing in heavy weather. Even in gale and storm conditions her motion is gentle, which translates to safer working conditions on deck and below. Even so, booms are always secured with preventers and are never allowed to swing uncontrolled across the deck.

9
Paean to Patagonia
(Deborah)

62 *Playing in Chilean Patagonia*
Dusky dolphins cavort as I row lines ashore in the Sarmiento Channel. They seem to be the only creatures in the world attracted to my singing...

Released from the clutch of the tide rip, *Northern Light* leaps forward into Chile's Chacao Channel. After three weeks of heavy ocean sailing, it is odd to feel the ocean swell diminish, and to find our bodies, so used to constant motion, delightfully wobbly on the still deck. I look forward to our first step onshore, since it will mark the end of the Roaring Forties passage, but for now I am content to breathe a good deep sigh at the proximity of land. How comforting it is to have land and springtime replace the ocean's assault on my senses. And how dramatically the richly oxygenated air and the sweet smell of flowers contrast to the salty sea mist of the last weeks.

It is a warm, tranquil Sunday, and the local people are taking advantage of it. The waterways are bustling with traffic, but there is no cargo in sight in the open boats. Everyone is going calling and taking as many family members and neighbors as can squeeze in. *Northern Light* is the only boat burning fossil fuel to make headway; all the Chilean boats are being rowed. Everyone between the ages of ten and eighty is pulling his weight, each on a single oar. The very young and very old wave as we pass; the rest simply smile.

We will not make it all the way to our port of entry before nightfall, so we drop the hook in a small cove off the main channel. My eyelids are heavy, but my grin is all the stronger, and I invite Rolf to sit with me on the foredeck and to drink in the sights surrounding our first Patagonian anchorage: flowering trees emblazoning the hills above a pebble beach, a small church, wide waterways and a backdrop of high Andean peaks. Land tantalizes us after the long passage, and we want to go ashore so badly that it is delicious not to.

For weeks now Rolf has been singing the praises of the Centolla, the southern king crab indigenous to the Chilean channels. He has induced mouthwatering anticipation, and as luck would have it, there are traps right in our anchorage. The old tender rows slowly past us on his way home and we trade a Norwegian fisherman's jacket for four huge crabs. We place the largest on the cupola. Its legs reach almost to the bottom edge of the plexiglass. One leg could be enough for a dinner portion. While Rolf is below boiling them and melting butter, I sit on deck watching the full moon rise over a snow-covered volcano, daydreaming like any spring-struck lover.

As our visit to Patagonia unfolds, I become convinced that it is my paradise on earth. It is the most wild, alive, testy, and spectacular place I have ever been. It is full of ultimates: the world's largest archipelago lying at the base of the youngest and longest mountain chain, with the biggest birds, the most helpful dolphins and the most delicious shellfish. As appreciative as I am, Rolf is more so. In Patagonia, he is in his element: all his skills will be drawn upon and the wilderness around him is the perfect answer to the call of his spirit.

In the northern part of the channels our cruising pattern is set. We stay put when the weather is bad, taking advantage of any short breaks in the rain to go ashore and hike. When a good day arrives, we go sailing. After all, we wouldn't want the spectacularly stern scenery to be obscured by the mist or fog or rainclouds. Before setting out, we mark the possible anchorages for the next 10–50 miles. We rule out most of the anchorages marked on the charts, since they have been recommended by large ships and are usually too deep, big and exposed for *Northern Light*. Instead, we look for coves surrounded by low topography with streams running into them. Streams deposit sediment at their mouths, which means we may find good holding near them in shallow water.

Underway we take turns: one of us perfects the gybe, the other cooks. Food is a passion-bordering-on-obsession in the chilly weather. It is only a month since we left the tropics; our bodies are adjusting and crave calories. We eat five meals a day to keep the fires stoked. We eat more all the

63 *Northern Light* against a glacier wall in Snowstorm Sound (Seno Ventisquero). She is probably one of a handful of boats ever to have entered this sound, as it is marked unnavigable on the chart. We searched painstakingly for a spot with enough water to allow us entry over the sandbar and, after bumping a few times, found one.

64 (following pages) Sailing in Snowstorm Sound, which we renamed Sound of Rain after four consecutive wet days, and renamed again The Garden of Eden when the sun came out.

time and yet get thinner—a gourmand's paradise! Out comes warmer clothing, but we choose not to pamper ourselves; we save the warmest pile clothing for the south and leave the heater turned off. Our bodies, especially our hands, respond by toughening to the cold, and we believe that in the long run our being used to the cold will lessen the likelihood of illness.

Entering a new anchorage is always exciting, but in Patagonia there is a special twist: dolphins pilot us in and show us where to drop the hook. These little guys often appear when we are about to enter an anchorage, attracted by the echo sounder, we assume. They streak to the bow, stay ahead of *Northern Light* if she is taking the correct course in, or gang up to port or starboard and "force" the bow one way or another when they want us to alter course. Then our underwater crewmates zoom ahead again, and above the spot where they recommend we drop the anchor, they begin to leap into the air, spinning or doing flips! We are not the only ones who have found the dolphins helpful. There is a native saying here that when dolphins whistle as they leap, a storm is coming and boats should take shelter. So, perhaps dolphins are responsible for the superstition of whistling up a storm.

Unfortunately, these dolphins won't accompany us south of the Antarctic Convergence, so Rolf and I use the time in Patagonia to perfect our anchoring teamwork and technique. This includes a variety of combinations of Rolf setting the anchor and me taking a line or lines ashore. The usual routine is: Rolf puts *Northern Light* in position and drops the anchor with five times the depth of chain. Meanwhile, I row the dinghy and a line ashore, attach the line around a tree or a rock, and let it pay out as I row back. With the anchor set, Rolf takes *Northern Light* in reverse to meet me, takes the end of the shore line, belays it and then winches up the slack in the anchor chain.

Once we get good enough at it to be effective in the dark, we make our first nighttime anchoring maneuver, practicing for Antarctica where there will also be no navigational aids to guide us. We turn out of the main channel toward a small bay. We proceed along a predetermined course toward shallow water. Rolf steers while I make sure the depthsounder readings match those on the chart. At the chosen depth, we drop the hook, inflate the dinghy, and take shore lines to a tree. It works well. But we also get our share of unplanned nighttime maneuvers; the holding in Patagonia is not the best in the world, and the gusts are especially strong.

Canal Chacao

Puerto Montt

Isla Chiloé

Canal Moraleda

Bahia Anna Pink

Golfo de Peñas

Patagonia

Chilean

ANDES MOUNTAINS

Canal Concepción

N

Estero Peel

Canal Sarmiento

Cabo Pilar

75 NM

65 *Squall in Beagle Channel*

66 *Ready for a gybe*

67 *Long day at the helm*

Williwaws
(Rolf)

Sailing through Chilean Patagonia, we must pay strict attention to the never-ending stream of depressions moving eastward across it or just to the south. South of 50°S, we add a lookout for williwaws, violent gusts that scream down the hills. They are created when the depressions' frontal systems meet the high topography.

When a warm front arrives from the South Pacific, only a gradual wind increase occurs. If the depression that follows is deep, the weather changes dramatically. As the cold front moves in over the offshore islands, their high peaks disturb the wind's flow. This turbulence creates eddies that may even affect the jetstream and drag it down the steep mountainsides to the water's surface.

A williwaw can come from anywhere; it is unrelated to the prevailing wind direction. The gust hits the water's surface, rips off the upper layer, tears it into fine spray, and within ten to fifteen seconds turns the spray into a wall for the wind to shovel ahead of it. As the wind and water plow through, we deal with winds exceeding 100 knots... especially dangerous if sails are up.

The first williwaw hit us when Deborah was aboard alone. I was off in the dinghy checking out a possible anchorage. The engine was in neutral when she first heard the distant roar. Looking for the source of the noise, she saw water being churned into whitecaps and hurled 100 feet into the air. She engaged the engine, turned *Northern Light* to face the force bow-on, then turned her own face away from the force of the blast.

65 Patagonian squalls differ from tropical or temperate-climate squalls. They are the result of strong winds or gales blowing at sea or thousands of feet above land. Clouds like this carry rain or snow and easily pack 40–80 knots of wind. In the channels we watch astern as much as ahead so as not to be surprised by them.

66 and 67 For two months in Chilean Patagonia we are regularly exposed to both cold and hard winds. We grow accustomed to the climate until we can work with bare hands in temperatures close to freezing point.

68 If there is nothing to attach shore lines to, we hammer removable pitons into cracks in the rock.

69 Shore lines hold the boat in position where we don't have much room to swing or where there is likely to be a strong offshore wind or williwaws. Two shore lines are required in some instances, as in this nook where *Northern Light* has no room to swing, because she is surrounded by shallow water and submerged rocks.

68 *Scandinavian removable boat piton*

69 *Stern to the wind in Peel Inlet*

Secure anchorages
(Rolf)

Because of the sudden weather changes and possibly violent storm conditions in Chilean Patagonia, it is important to locate—or to create—safe anchorages. So that we do not find ourselves out in the narrow waterways after dark, we follow these guidelines: we choose the next harbor before we trip anchor, and we make certain to be halfway there before noon. Since the morning's weather seldom lasts the entire day, we also mark alternative retreats.

The best harbors are surrounded by low land where we can take stern lines ashore into the wind. The lower the upwind cliffs, the steadier the wind is. The stronger the wind, the steadier *Northern Light* hangs in her shore lines and the less strain the anchor takes while keeping the bow still.

When high land surrounds a harbor, there is a greater risk of violent down drafts and williwaws from any direction. If we anchor in such a place and take shore lines, it is likely that the wind will hit from abeam, causing the boat to drag. If we are forced to let the shore lines go and swing on the anchor, the risks are that the anchor chain will wrap around rocks on the bottom, or the boat will drag and drift away into deeper water, with the anchor hanging uselessly straight down, or the boat will run aground. If it is pitch black outside, with the rain pouring so hard that the land's contour is obliterated—then we get a very poor start that day.

In Peel Inlet we anchor and take stern lines ashore. The surroundings not only provide good shelter from wind and sea, they also present us with a magnificent view of the Andes and of a mighty glacier, its mile-long ice wall rising 180 feet high a mile away from us across open water. If the good weather lasts, the morning sun will transform this panorama into one of the most spectacular we have seen.

On the way to this anchorage we passed by the glacier wall. I saw that it had receded approximately 900 feet from the position it occupied five years ago when I was last here. There was also less ice floating in the bay. Five years ago ice pieces covered the water two miles out into the channel; now they float out only 500 feet in front of the wall. The glacier that then was very active and often calved icebergs is now quiet. We don't hear as much as a single crack.

At 2000 hours the first rumble peels away from the glacier. Just after dark *Northern Light* starts rolling; the motion is like a swell from a big ship passing. For a long time we sit on deck listening. Each hour, as the rumbling increases, the swells that make the boat tug at her shore lines become more frequent. By late night the anchorage is no longer safe, but we cannot move until daylight. In the first rays of morning light we see that the ice not only reaches us, it covers the water's surface as far as it did five years earlier.

The glaciers in Chile normally advance 9–15 feet a day. In this single night the glacier moved 100 feet, discharging 2,200,000 cubic yards of ice. Fast advances like this one—surges—can last as long as six months and move the glacier's ice wall forward three miles. We leave, picking our way out gingerly.

70 *Condor's view of Sarmiento Channel*

Onshore in Patagonia
(Deborah)

We are lucky with the weather during our six-week stay in Patagonia; it only drenches us about half of the time. Neither Rolf nor I find the rain dismal or gloomy since we love the results: rainbows, lakes and streams, waterfalls, thick lush vegetation, plenty of the best-tasting water in the world and an abundance for freshwater baths.

At every possible opportunity between rain showers, we go ashore to stretch our legs and explore. If the boat is secure in her anchorage and the weather is fine, we pack a picnic and leave for the day. Hiking in this wild and woolly country, foothills to the Andes, provides us with continual surprises and the pleasure of discovering wildlife and vegetation we have never seen before.

In the northernmost and populated part of the archipelago, the land is cleared and farmed. We follow cow paths mostly, wandering around the hillsides and stopping to chat with people we meet. Not much farther south, the vegetation becomes impenetrably dense. Since the high-tide mark becomes the boundary of explorable territory, I start treasure hunting, collecting shells and rocks. I vow to Rolf that I will stop before *Northern Light's* waterline disappears.

South of the heavy rain belt there is less vegetation, and we scale the hills like outrageously happy and healthy goats. We are training hard for the south ice, knowing that every bit of physical strength will be drawn upon there and that our top physical condition will translate to endurance and good spirit. It gets a bit ridiculous perhaps, when we

start to fight over who gets to pump the anchor aboard... but the deeper the anchorage, the more challenge it is to bring aboard the 45-pound CQR plow anchor and 1/2″ chain without pausing.

As we progress into summertime, the days lengthen, and our chances of getting onshore or at least off the boat increase. We often row the dinghy to explore the perimeter of our anchorage. It is fantastic at low tide, when the molluscs are exposed: the primitive chiton with their plated shells, limpets, and the blue mussels—which we love to steam for dinner. Rowing has another advantage: it doesn't startle the birds, and we can get close for a good gander at them.

The season also facilitates our birdwatching. Since their eggs have hatched, many birds must remain on the ground to protect their young. From a distance we observe them, the rower through the binoculars, the other through a telephoto lens. My favorite for beauty is the kelp goose. The male is pure white, the female wears a brown and white herringbone suit splashed with emerald green, and the chick is fluffy gray down. These geese eat kelp and sea lettuce exposed at low tide and therefore have a linear beach territory where they graze. The first time we see a family we watch them from another island. The following day while we are immobilized, working on our big red baby, they come much closer than we had dared—to people-watch.

As unobtrusive as we try to be, we are intruders in the

Cabo Pilar

Estrecho de Magallanes

N

Tierra
del Fuego

'The Furious Fifties'   Puerto Hope

Seno Ocasión   Canal Beagle

SOUTH PACIFIC   Seno
    Ventisquero

OCEAN

Cabo de
Hornos

60 NM   DRAKE PASSAGE

70 Less dense vegetation surrounding Sarmiento Channel allows day-long hikes in the mountains.

71 I get the chance to unwind and play ashore in Hope Harbor.

72 Patagonia is an easy place to keep the water tanks topped up. Here, in Balandra Cove, Rolf accomplishes this chore at low tide when he can also harvest blue mussels for dinner.

73 Under the canopy of a maritime forest at the edge of the Beagle Channel, I savor the light and protection from the wind. It is the last time for many months that I can enjoy greenery. Relaxing, I drift away in thought.

wild, and the wildlife does not have prepared responses for us. The steamer duck is a bird that cannot fly; its wings have evolved for use underwater, to dive for shellfish. On the surface, it uses them for propulsion by whirling them like the paddle wheels of a steam wheeler. When startled, it paddles at "heart-attack" speed in whatever direction it happens to be pointed and continues endlessly. It is an appropriate response to get away from another steamer, but not from its new big "enemy." It often paddles right across our path and continues much farther than it needs to escape from us. It is a comical sight but weighs on my heart.

Patagonia's heavy winds are used to advantage by two of the world's heaviest birds. While the channels are visited by the albatross, the largest globe-circling seabird and the one with the biggest wingspan, the Andes Mountains are the home of the Andean condor, the largest flying land bird in the world and the one with the largest wing area.

We have been watching the albatross ever since we reached 40° South, marveling at its soaring techniques, especially against the wind. Now when we leave the beaten track through the archipelago and come to the edge of the mainland, we see the condor. As I am picking berries on the moraine of a receding glacier, I notice about ten of these birds of prey circling in a thermal above me. I point them out to Rolf, and we wait, hoping they will come closer. Since I have had the most success in attracting birds' attention on this voyage, Rolf elicits my help to bring his photographic subjects closer. I do the best imitation of the dying swan that a klutz can. Condors must find swans tasty; in no time, they are circling down, down, descending on us. They are huge, and ultimately I am glad that my smell is not appetizing to them.

Some of our daytrips consist of exploration by dinghy and hiking. We go as far up a stream or river as possible and then explore on foot as far as the vegetation permits. We watch kingfishers, examine the lichens, moss and fungi, trees dwarfed by and bowing to the wind, marshy areas dripping with slime and gook, and bogs alive with bizarre caterpillars and the familiar frog. Nearly every time we return from a foray ashore we pull books from their shelves to try to identify the things we've seen. Each time we succeed, we feel as though we are walking through a museum of fine art, unveiling masterpiece after masterpiece.

Our time in Patagonia leaves us feeling fresh and vital and filled to the brim with new impressions of this magnificent planet. We are also healthy and fit, and rough and ready for Antarctica.

71 *Joy in Hope Harbor*

72 *... and blue mussels for dinner*

73 *Private time*

57

74 *Sea lions in Beagle Channel*
75 *Too windy in Ocasion Sound for anything to grow*

76 *Romanche Glacier*

74 These sea lions climb up onto rocks at high tide to rest and digest their food in safety. They inhabit the northwest arm of the Beagle Channel, a more temperate climate zone than the tempestuous coastline just to the west.

75 The Pilot Book warns: ''Violent and unpredictable squalls are frequent in the area south of 50° South and are particularly hazardous on the W and SW coasts.'' The result of the fierce winds and driving rains in this sub-Antarctic climate zone is barren rocks like these in Ocasion Sound at 54°30'S where 30 percent of winds are Force 7 or more. The few trees and shrubs that can exist in the heavy winds are dwarfed and creep along the rocks horizontally.

76 The Beagle Channel is one of the most scenic waterways in the world, with high glaciated mountains on its northern side. Romanche Glacier is the only icefall in the channel with a tandem waterfall. A water ''avalanche'' occurs while we sail past, preceded by the same thunderous explosion of an ice wall calving, and torrentially doubles the waterfall for a few minutes.

10
On the edge

(Deborah)

77 *Cape Horn*

For the last two weeks, deep depressions have been pummeling Tierra del Fuego with winds up to 95 knots. We work our way slowly toward Cape Horn and wait for the optimum moment to leave the protection of the inland waterways, but we never anticipated getting this northeasterly breeze... there is less than a 10 percent chance of such a wind direction.

I am an ordinary person in an extraordinary situation. Cape Horn, my ultimate goal, is metamorphosing into a landmark. A consummate moment, it is the point from which both finish and start radiate; I feel as close to infinity as is humanly possible. I look back to the cliff one final time to forever lock in every nuance. I will always be able to close my eyes and see, hear, and feel the scene: sailing past a diamond in the rough.

The water under our keel at this moment has claimed the lives of thousands of sailors. Imagine their bravery. Not many years before square-rigged vessels first rounded the Horn, the Strait of Magellan was believed to be the boundary between earth and hell. No one dared sail farther south. When they did, they must have suffered. Approaching the Horn from long passages, they had no way to pick decent weather, as we did coming from the inland waterways. They had to face whatever they met, in ships that went poorly to weather and that carried shifting cargo. They had to climb, clinging to treacherously icy rigging to take in and to set sail, eke meager sustenance from moldy food, and face the fury of the wind, sea and cold without the advan-

78 *The warm front brings increasing wind*

tage of modern clothing and foul-weather gear. I doubt that many of us, as pampered as we are, could survive such circumstances.

When I pay silent homage to those who lost their lives in the waters of this Cape, the cliff assumes the morose appearance of a huge gravestone. It is a memorial to men I only met in books. But their stories were the most impressive that I, as an eight-year-old who had never set eyes on the ocean, had ever read. Playing make-believe, I wanted to re-enact the heroic scenes of struggle and adventure on the high seas. My treehouse became my ship and Cape Horn the destination. I invited my three brothers to come along. But from their "boys only" treehouse and game of Cowboys and Indians, they laughed and shot at me. Since no one would share my vision of Cape Horn, it submerged. In solitude, I returned to the books. I've been sailing toward this moment ever since.

Now, with the Cape astern, we are out. Patagonia, spectacular Patagonia, is behind us, and Antarctica lies ahead. We are entering the realm of the White Continent, the earth's most powerful weather machine. It controls us now, and until we cross this latitude on our homeward journey it will keep our reality in constant transition. Cranking out depressions on the average of every thirty-six hours, spinning them away on variable and unpredictable tracks, and without the usual warning of barometric change, it leaves us with one constant: no safety. In Antarctica, we will never be secure in an anchorage. Gale force winds will shift unpredictably during the night and could force us into areas choked with icebergs.

But there are more immediate problems facing us now. The passing depressions and frontal troughs are also a serious concern in Drake Passage, notorious bottleneck of the Furious Fifties, known for its huge waves. If a fast and furious wind shift crosses these waves—called "graybeards"—and results in furious cross-seas, we may experience freak waves. A freak wave can be twice as high as the existing waves, or its trough twice as deep. Or it can be triangular or conical-shaped or have a vertical face. It can knock a boat down on its side or farther, or flip it end-over-end. Knockdown or pitchpole, and wind above a level of manageability, are what I fear now. And these are not the imagined dangers or the ungrounded fears of the novice.

We strive to trim to the changes inherent in this fluid environment. There is no doubt that we have prepared the boat as best we can in light of grim weather statistics and in anticipation of heavy weather in Drake Passage. Every-

thing is in good working order; we have paid constant attention to the boat over the 24,000 miles we covered to get here from Sweden. Furthermore, *Northern Light* is as sealed as a steel drum; she will take a pitchpole, a knockdown or a capsize without flooding the interior. The only difference between her and a washing machine is that the washing machine keeps its water inside.

To avoid personal injury in heavy weather, we have secured or stowed everything heavy or sharp. Our living area is stark; the homey atmosphere is gone. Only soft clothing remains on the shelves. Lockers and floorboards are bolted or screwed shut. It will make our daily "food shopping" more tedious, but it is preferable to being killed by a flying canned chicken. Imagine having to explain that to my mother.

Our nose is out into Drake Passage, and the wind is slowly and steadily increasing. Knowing the Pilot Book statistics by heart and having them continually run through my mind winds the edginess one turn tighter. The external world becomes edged by a corona and is matched internally by a kernel of equal brilliance that threatens to spread, consuming me in the process: an emptiness that will void me, nullify me... a blinding white anxiety. Never do I speak of this dread to my partner. Maintaining silence is a way of securing privacy onboard. I do it for myself so I can work it out my own way, and I do it for Rolf, to spare him additional worry. As captain, he has plenty already. Indeed, all that Rolf perceives is that I am quiet and seem to enjoy my deckwork, albeit robotically.

Neither of us has sea legs after ten weeks in the channels, so we decide to shorten watches to two or three hours. *Northern Light* continues on course, steered by our third crewmate, the trusty windsteering. After eighteen hours the wind eases and begins to shift through North; we gybe. When it reaches West, we change sail, dropping the genoa and hoisting the working jib I and the staysail. Then as the wind rapidly increases, we perform in double time the following ballet: take a reef in the main, drop the jib, take a reef in the mizzen, drop the main, drop the mizzen. Our fit physical condition pays off, so does our rehearsed choreography, and so does *Northern Light*. Long-keeled, ketch-rigged, double-ender, she is a heavy-weather dreamboat, taking 60 knots on the beam and making 7 knots under staysail alone.

When Rolf wakes me for my next watch, he informs me that I've just slept through the strongest gusts he's ever experienced at sea. It's a treasured boat that affords rest to the crew in situations like these. But even in sleep my fear has not dwindled, and holding in the tension has caused physical pain in my chest.

I climb the ladder and sit there, looking out of the plexi-glass dome. It is midday, dark and blowing. The seas are heavily crested and slamming the hull occasionally. I absorb the present patterns and their sounds so that I can perceive change, especially sustained wind that builds waves too big to take abeam or a wind decrease that would catch us with too little sail. When all is noted, and between my normal watch responsibilities, I begin my usual exercise/massage routine, trying to regain grace. I crave release from the knot that's lived just under my ribcage off and on for the two years since we've planned this route and that has reached an unbearable proportion in the last twenty-four hours. The Greeks believed that this spot is the body's emotional center. Perhaps they were right; massaging it makes me puke. It is not motion sickness I have been suffering from, it is emotion sickness. The release spreads.

My ordeal of anticipation is finally ending. After all, in twenty-four hours not only have we covered half the distance to the closest Antarctic anchorage, in Deception Is-land, but we have maintained a course west of south—an optimum course to proceed much farther to the south on the Peninsula. I have slept through the worst that this depression had to offer. Rolf's theory of keeping speed in heavy weather has worked again. *Northern Light* can handle a lot more than this. So can Rolf. So can I.

When Rolf gets up, I tell him about the fear that I have held inside for so long. The truth dictates that I now let it go; I shed a few tears and get a long hug. Within the hour, the wind begins to die down. Lunch gets cold while we set more sail. I feel fine; I can eat and rest better, and I begin to feel like my old self. Or perhaps, I should say like a new self—one that has faced a deep-seated dread that was not altogether realistic yet real to me and undeniably under my skin all those years. And now, finally finished, wiped clean, played out.

79 *Sheeting in a rainbow*
When you pass beyond the stage of reacting fearfully to an ocean in storm conditions, the inner capacity to perceive beauty and pleasure reappears.

80 While working on deck in heavy weather, we spend as much time as possible on the windward side—the high, dry, safe side. During a tack, Rolf is forced to work on the lee side in order to free a running backstay that had jammed.

81 At night, it is important to know where the handholds are and crucial to know where every line is belayed.

Each line has its own cleat. The system exists so that neither of us has to fumble around searching for a halyard or sheet. A mistaken change from the established routine could lead to catastrophic consequences. If the wrong line is belayed on a cleat, and we free it during a maneuver, something unexpected will happen. Dam-

age could be done to the rigging, and we could easily get hurt or pulled over the side.

From this point on we use neoprene diving gloves while making sail changes in heavy weather. Even though hands are wet inside, they stay warm, which provides better protection and more comfort than the combination of woolen mittens/rubber mitts.

Don't go overboard
(Rolf)

Co-ordinated work on deck and rigid discipline are the most important safety principles on *Northern Light*. Safety harnesses don't stop accidents from happening; they change the result, and then only if the harnesses are designed correctly and used correctly. Each of our safety harnesses is attached to a 6-foot line with two snap-hooks: one in the middle and one at the end. During deck work either can be hooked to one of two wires that run from the cockpit to the bowsprit on either side of the mast. When hooked in properly it is impossible to go overboard.

In 32°F water we can only expect to have a few minutes of survival time without a survival suit. During a solo watch, the difference is marginal between falling overboard without a lifeline and falling overboard at the end of a too-long tether. In the first instance you would simply disappear in the dark; in the second case the body would bang against the topsides, at best disturbing the night's sleep of the other who so badly needs rest.

80 *Running backstays have good and bad points*

81 *Time to drop the working jib*

11
Beyond the known world

(Rolf)

82 *A tabular iceberg, 120 feet high, with hangar-sized caves*

83 *Antarctic Convergence at 61°30′ South*

In the first thirty-six hours after leaving Tierra del Fuego, we changed sail combinations nineteen times. For four hours we endured hurricane-force gusts that whipped the waves into so much spray that the visible border between water and air disappeared. Twelve hours later we were becalmed.

Now we lie on a calm sea for the second time in twenty-four hours, sails down, waiting for wind. It is a short holiday for us, and we take full advantage of it. The skylights are open, and the boat is airing. I lie on deck in the sunshine and hope that my socks, rubber boots and wool sweater will have time to dry out before the wind carousel starts spinning full speed again.

The weather changes here are nearly brutal. Reaching the Antarctic Convergence at 61°30′S, we cross into colder Antarctic water, and the sun's fiery disc is closed out by fog. Moisture runs in rivulets down the sails and rigging. We stand shivering in the cold damp air as our bodies struggle to adjust to the new environment. Since yesterday, the water temperature has dropped from 40–45°F to around freezing, and it will drop to 28°F at our most southerly position along the Antarctic Peninsula.

We can't lock out the cold, and the only heating system

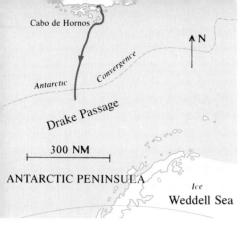

Cabo de Hornos
Antarctic Convergence
Drake Passage
300 NM
ANTARCTIC PENINSULA
Ice
Weddell Sea
N

82 and 83 In Drake Passage we measure water temperature to ascertain where we meet the colder Antarctic surface stream. We find this Antarctic Convergence 100 miles farther south than marked on the Pilot Chart. Continuing south we must expect tabular icebergs at any time.

84 The Convergence marks an impenetrable barrier to many life forms.

Albatrosses nest north of the Convergence but freely cross the border in search of food. They stop at the ice, where the wind and wave action and therefore their soaring ability diminishes.

85 Cape pigeons prefer to stay in the rich feeding areas south of the Convergence in the summer.

86 We see whales moving south to their summer feeding grounds, but the dolphins turn around at the Convergence and swim back northward.

we have is the stove/oven. Our heater can't be run. Although it is in working order, we couldn't find kerosene in South America with the proper flamepoint. The oven will warm the navigation area to around 50°F. Beyond that, Deborah and I will have to rely upon our bodies' own capacities and resources to keep warm.

South of the Convergence, we once again encounter iceberg risk, with poor visibility. And there is an additional danger: the icebergs breaking away from the Antarctic ice shelves are much bigger than those calving from glaciers. We can't expect to skirt icebergs here, changing course a mere 10–15 degrees to avoid them; the tabular icebergs that move northeast along the Antarctic Peninsula and through Drake Passage can be so large that both ends disappear into the fog. They more resemble coastlines; we may have to make at least a 90-degree turn to avoid them. Even with good visibility it may be impossible to judge which way is best to turn to get around them.

Whether the gigantic iceberg sighted off South Georgia in 1977 broke off from the Ross Ice Shelf and went through Drake Passage, or broke off from the ice shelf in the Weddell Sea is not known, but the fact that it was 90 miles long is a clear warning. We need an avoidance plan especially designed for heavy weather, low visibility, and tabular icebergs. We decide to use sail combinations at all times which will allow us, in less than the visible distance, to tack or gybe *Northern Light* and beat our way free. That is, if we can beat free.

The worst possible scenario I can imagine places us in very strong wind and resulting high seas. Then we could *only* sail downwind and could not possibly turn beam to the sea to avoid an iceberg. Happily, the farther south we go, the less likely it is that this dangerous combination will occur. A majority of the depressions' centers plow through Drake Passage, following the latitudes 60–62°S, and it is the front to the north of the center that creates the heaviest wind.

Even so, it is with great apprehension that we continue south to take our first stumbling steps into the totally new world of the Antarctic Ocean. Indigenous life forms are suited to the environment and remain so through an ongoing selection process. As visitors, our survival will depend upon our own ability to analyze and continually act and react appropriately to the new environment. It will test our ingenuity. Only a voyage into space could make my heart beat faster.

84 *Black-browed albatross*

85 *Cape pigeon*

86 *Hourglass dolphin*

12
The last continent

(Rolf)

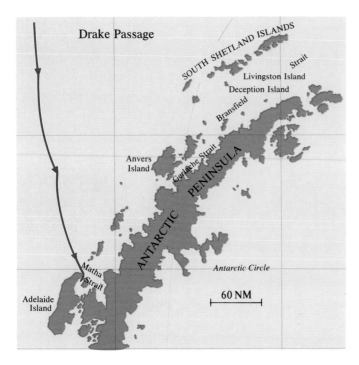

Two-and-a-half days after crossing the Antarctic Convergence we sail over the continental shelf 60 miles off the Antarctic Peninsula. In two hours the water shoals up from 12,000 feet to 1,200 feet. In a navigational sense we have already arrived at Antarctica—and to all the area's uncertainties.

In our planning, there has been so much conjecture, and so many ifs and alternatives. Some will soon be blotted out as others are transformed into reality. The prospect is thrilling.

We have been keeping a strict iceberg watch since crossing the Convergence, and the fact that we haven't yet seen one iceberg makes us wonder if the coastal ice situation here will be similar to what we found in Greenland: free water all the way to land and then an impenetrable ice barrier blocking our destination, Matha Strait. Or, is it simply a year with little ice?

One thing we know for certain: if we do make it in, we won't have much use for the Antarctic Pilot's few anchorage recommendations. The listings read like this: "... anchorage can be obtained off the smaller island, at a depth of 120−180 feet. The bottom is rocky, the holding is poor, and there is a great risk of fouling the anchor. Strong

tidal streams transport huge quantities of ice through the anchorage, which is not recommended."

As we sail into more shallow water, the ocean changes character. For the last twenty-four hours, even though high, the seas from the 15-knot northeast wind were long and gentle. Now as they meet the opposing 1−1.5-knot coastal current, they become very short and steep, rising as high as 12−15 feet. Additionally, a remnant swell from the west intersects the line almost at a right angle.

On our south-southeast course we are in the grip of the old swell from abeam on the lee side. It makes *Northern Light* roll, and when she rolls heavily the sails lose air completely. Seconds later she rolls back and the sails fill—with a bang. The strain is hard on the sail cloth, so I replace the old, weak genoa with the newer, highcut yankee. Just as I finish the fifteen-minute job of changing headsails, the wind dies completely.

When the boat speed diminishes in these turbulent seas, it becomes chaotic onboard. The boat pitches and rolls so violently that the flopping sails can no longer do their job. I start to drop all of them.

I find this to be the most difficult working condition on deck, when there is no constant rhythm to the boat's motion. When the yankee is halfway down, its halyard catches on the port spreader. As I leave the bowsprit to try to free it, a breaking sea washes the sail over the side. While I'm dragging the sail back up on deck, the boat rolls, and the halyard catches the other spreader. From below-decks I hear something heavy hitting the floorboards and rolling back and forth.

When I get all the sails down and secured, the wind picks up from northeast and I have to reverse my work, thankfully with less hassle. When I go below to check the situation there, Deborah tells me that a 50-pound bag of pumpkins had come undone in the mad motion. The bag had been perfectly secured to withstand both gale and storm, but this had been too much. We laugh as Deborah recounts her efforts to retrieve the rolling pumpkins.

There will be no more sleep from this point forward. Deborah and I both want to absorb the final hours of approach to Antarctica, as our dream unfolds and our questions are answered. At the end of my watch I notice it darkening just off the port bow. But I know land is still 30 miles away and impossible to see in this visibility. When I start to be aware of a shifting blue tone in the otherwise gray surroundings, I know I am looking at an iceberg, more gigantic than any I have ever seen.

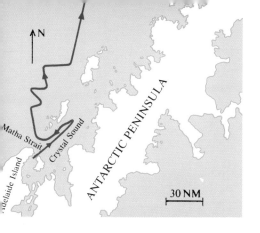

87 Landfall in Antarctica is more exciting than any other on earth. It is impossible to make proper surveys because of the ice, which means that undiscovered shoals can exist where the chart shows deep water. That aside, we cannot be certain that we will reach any anchorage that we have found on the chart—any entrance can be plugged by a giant iceberg.

87 *The Antarctic Peninsula—once connected to the Andes*

The berg is so huge that it has its own weather system. To windward the wind builds a bright white condensation cloud that rises along the entire slab-shaped side. To leeward the wind dies. The world is quiet. The only thing that we hear is the swell's boom as it smashes against the obstacle.

The iceberg is moving at a speed exceeding one knot. Its momentum is beyond my comprehension; there is nothing we human beings have created that can stop its motion. For me the mammoth iceberg is illusory, half way between in-

animate material and a living essence. Very soon we see more icebergs. One looks like a hand, holding up a finger as a warning sign. Another looks like a grotesque Indonesian temple figure.

We keep course toward Matha Strait and have only a couple of miles to go to reach the entrance to the archipelago north of Adelaide Island when the fog curtain slowly lifts. Out of the sea rises a line of 6,000-foot-high peaks covered with ice and snow.

This majestic landscape deflates our preconceived notions about Antarctica. We had anticipated that after enduring thousands of years of snowstorms, the coldest continent on earth would be blindingly white. Instead we are presented with shimmering color. Only a couple of fingers above the horizon, the slowly setting sun sends narrow beams of light onto the glaciers' snowfields, causing them to shift in color from purple to green, yellow, orange and red. Ironically, only white is missing.

Very soon after the sunset, two perpendicular fire columns shoot up from the ocean, rising 5−10 degrees above the horizon. The distance between them equals the sun's diameter. It is a color flash crescendo−sun pillars−a climax seen only in the southern polar region. My mind goes blank. Deborah is silent. We are spellbound.

Crossing south over the Antarctic Circle I feel I am going through the kind of change that only those who have risked disaster to reach an unknown destination and succeeded can know. I sense a special freedom, an explorer's privileged rebirth.

We turn south in Crystal Sound, heading east of Adelaide Island. The wind dies completely, and all the swell disappears. The first, exciting stage is over. We feel how tired and hungry we are, so we drop the sails and go down into the galley to make something hot to eat. Finding an anchorage is a problem for the future; considering the favorable ice situation and the bright nights, we can sail twenty-four hours a day.

In order not to exhaust ourselves we decide that after dinner one of us should sleep for a while. I pull the shorter straw and come up on deck just as a fresh southeasterly wind reaches us. I set the yankee II, which is still hanked on the forestay. Under it alone we make 7−8 knots.

We have decided to make for a harbor in the north. Ahead of us I see a band of ice coming out from a glacier on the right. I am not able to leave the helm for long, but I dive down to the navigation desk to study the chart before we reach the mass. As long as it doesn't get too tricky, I will let Deborah sleep. Since we don't know when we will reach a safe anchorage it is important that at least one of us is in reasonable shape.

It takes more than an hour before we get enough ice-free water for me to return to the chart table. However I try, I can't get the navigation to agree with what I see around us. According to the chart there should be ten small islands inside a 2-by-2-mile area to starboard, but according to my eyes they are not there.

For a while I believe that because I am unused to the

enormous scale I have misjudged the distances. I also know I am very tired, but I haven't yet had a problem thinking clearly and logically. Can we be in a local magnetic anomaly that I don't know about? Or...

I go no further in my attempt to figure out where we are. Ahead is a new ice-congested area that makes it impossible for me to concentrate any longer on the navigation. I must give all my attention to boat handling. I must wake Deborah; I can't sail any longer without verifying our position. If I have steered the wrong course, we will be aground on a shoal in just 2 miles.

When Deborah comes up on deck she is surprised to see how much the wind has increased. She had been sleeping so deeply that she never even heard me setting sail. She is also surprised to see the extent of the ice around us and remarks: "Sooner or later, you will have to rest, and I don't think that I can sail the boat myself safely in so much ice."

She understands that I need immediate help and takes the helm. I must figure out where we are. It doesn't take more than a few minutes before Deborah says: "Rolf, we can't continue into this ice jam in so much wind! We shouldn't stubbornly cling to our original plan of searching for an anchorage. We have to turn around and leave to get sea room."

She's right. I realize that immediately. I was too tired to look objectively at the evolving reality. The point that pleases me is the value and trust I now have in Deborah's knowledge and judgement. We hoist the mizzen with one reef and set the staysail. In the tack, I drop the yankee II and tie it to the lifeline. The wind is steadily increasing; it's now blowing 38 knots. Ahead of us we have a hard, close reach to get out to sea.

Deborah can't fathom the idea that I wasn't clear in my navigation and she searches for the islands I couldn't find. Just as we have given up hope of figuring out why I couldn't determine our position, the answer appears. When we see that an "island" we passed yesterday is actually an iceberg, we realize that conversely the entire group of small islands we had been looking for are now obscured by icebergs that have run over them.

As Deborah frees me from my watch, I begin to mull over the situation. I wonder if this is the end of our voyage to Antarctica. If it isn't possible to identify landmarks positively, how will we navigate safely? If the small islands where we had hoped to anchor are run over by icebergs, where will we find shelter? And I disappear down in sleep−four wonderful hours−until it's time to take over again.

89 In Antarctica the weather changes occur faster than anywhere else on earth. The sailor who hasn't found shelter, anchored in a safe place, or moved into ice-free water before the storm hits, can expect profound problems.

90 In spite of lack of sleep, Deborah has no problem staying awake while seas of ice-cold water continuously wash the tiredness off her face.

91 I try to figure out just one reason why we have sailed to Antarctica.

92 With mizzen and main sheeted in and the staysail backed, *Northern Light* lies hove-to along the Antarctic Peninsula.

89 *Storm brewing*

Heave-to retreat

In the late afternoon we experience the fourth shockingly fast weather change in one day. The barometer rushes downward, and the pressure change is accompanied by 48- to 55-knot storm gusts. The screaming in the rigging makes it impossible to try to talk to each other on deck. Only the sea's rumbling can overlay the wind's nerve-wracking din. Below, Deborah and I have to shout to each other.

Although irritating, noise itself is no danger. We may experience discomfort, but knowing that the boat can withstand a lot more abuse, we do not perceive natural forces as a threat to our safety. However, to stay on deck requires will-power, determination and stamina. Strong gusts whip our faces when we look forward. In the worst gusts, it is impossible to hold our eyes open to see if we have ice or free water ahead.

Around 2200, when dusk comes in tandem with a drop in visibility to a wavelength, we decide to heave-to. To do so we drop the headsail as we tack, and, without resheeting the staysail, double-reefed mainsail, and single-reefed mizzen, we bring *Northern Light* to a halt.

One of *Northern Light*'s design considerations, taken from the old Norwegian pilot boats designed by Colin Archer in the late 1800s, is the capacity for heaving-to comfortably. Even in storm conditions she can lie 60−70 degrees off the wind, taking the sea in the gentlest way possible, considering the circumstances. This motion makes it possible for us to cook, to rest and to live in a way which isn't possible in many other boats, even big ships, which roll and pitch heavily in storms.

With the sails set like this in a hove-to position, it is possible for us to make speed through the water in less than a minute. This is a crucial capability, since we might have to avoid an object in our path or move for something overtaking us, such as tabular icebergs that come from the ice-shelf in the Ross Sea, drifting north along the Antarctic Peninsula.

The difference between our speed and the icebergs' can be as much as 2 knots. In the present poor visibility it wouldn't take more than four minutes from the time we first sight a berg until it rams us—if we don't move. But as guests in their home waters, we plan to give right-of-way to even those icebergs that are overtaking us.

90 *It feels colder when you're tired*

91 *Blinded by sleet*

92 *Hove-to*

13
The gate opens
(Deborah)

93 *An Adélie penguin heralds our re-entry to Antarctica*

Never before have I been glad to be in a gale, but being hove-to lets us rest and recover from our first draining encounter with the White Continent. The glimpse of Antarctica was colored in shades of pastel and peril, intensified by novelty. Time spent in the gale is a comforting return to the familiar.

Now, with the northeaster diminishing, we move *Northern Light* out of her standby position and begin our second approach to Antarctica. As we steer due east toward Bismarck Strait and the shelter of land, the wind drops and the sky begins to clear. Only monstrous tabular icebergs are visible until we reach the edge of the continental shelf, when the ice-blanketed mountain peaks reappear. We near the belt of offshore islets, rocks, and ice that look like orbiting asteroids, and the calm extends its welcome feeling the way it did the first time.

I have learned from Odysseus, however, and do not trust appearances. In tandem with the calm is quiet but not peace; the vision is too dynamic. The scenery holds its limit of captured frozen energy, and it is doubled in the mirror image on the still water. It glitters too much, and the craggy, jagged rough motif is repeated too often. That other

factors are missing makes it all the more foreign. It is too sterile; there is no smell, no sound, no life. The sunshine makes no difference... this is a frozen land... and the cold is a powerful enemy.

Then the first sign of life appears. An Adélie penguin, the most formally dressed of the penguin family, calls out its greeting from an iceberg where it is taking a break from fishing. Suddenly everything changes. This penguin elevates my mood just as the sight of an albatross or dolphin has done in heavy weather. We will work hard finding them, but I know there will be treasures here.

It's time to search for our first anchorage. We motor cautiously around and between the ice, trying to keep to the track that is suggested for big ships with deeper draft than *Northern Light*'s. All the while we watch the depth-sounder. Charts of Antarctica are not to be trusted; a piece of ice may have hidden a shallow spot when the soundings were taken.

Faraday Islands appear to be a good place to look for shelter. This is a small, tightly clustered group which we believe will offer protection from drifting ice in any wind direction. What we don't expect is that in addition to the great shelter we will find greater companionship; Faraday is the site of a British Antarctic Survey station.

From their dinghy dock, a blond man directs us to the farthest cove, which is filled with fast ice. We break our way in a bit and then proceed to take shore lines. Rolf spends an hour to set two eyebolts in the rotten rock. It has been a long day. We forego a visit to the base in favor of a hot meal and rest, sweet uninterrupted rest.

We spend the next five days in the company of the twelve men who keep the station operational and record meteorological data. It's downright embarrassing at the beginning; I am so overwhelmed by having completed the passage, by the beauty and power of the rugged landscape that encircles their station, and last but not least, from hearing English from twelve strangers, that I am reduced to mumbling a chorus of "wows" to everything they tell us. Eventually, they tease me back into coherence.

They kindly explain their scientific work and any peculiarities of Antarctica they know will be of interest to us. For instance, they point out that as long as they have been studied, there has not been any pattern found to the tidal ebb and flow. They also share their wealth of information about the flora and fauna of the immediate area. Everyone is keenly interested in the wildlife; they are able to explain all sorts of bird and mammal behavior to us. We are warned

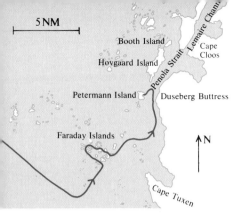

Booth Island
Hovgaard Island
Petermann Island
Faraday Islands
Penola Strait
Lemaire Channel
Cape Cloos
Duseberg Buttress
Cape Tuxen
N

94 *Northern Light* sails in the Penola Strait, with Duseberg Buttress on the Antarctic mainland as backdrop. Since the mainland's coast is steep-to along the Peninsula, we doubt that we will ever be able to land there.

95 (following pages) The spectacular Lemaire Channel with Booth Island and its cock's-comb ridge on the left and Cape Cloos on the right. The mountains behind the boat appear deceptively close but are actually 25 miles away.

that much of the wildlife is not particularly titillated by the presence of humans, and we get pointers about keeping safe distance, especially to the leopard seal.

The base is renamed Faraway Yacht Club while we are there. We did not expect social events in Antarctica, and these first few convivial days make a big difference to our morale.

While a high-pressure cell prevails over the Antarctic Peninsula we leave Faraday for Petermann Island, 5 miles to the north. We can't help but sail a little farther; Lemaire

94 *Penola Strait*

Channel, a narrow and spectacular split between the mainland and Booth Island beckons us. We circle around at the mouth and head for our anchorage, a small inlet on the eastern side of Petermann.

The inlet is very exposed to northeast winds, so we decide to tie *Northern Light* in place with shore lines fore and aft. It is soon accomplished, but not without the notice of a local gentoo penguin resident that swims in circles around the boat staring at this big red thing that appeared while it was out fishing.

We take shore lines fore and aft to the snow-free cliffs. *Northern Light* rests in a calm little inlet, but only 200 yards away icebergs are continuously drifting north at 0.5–1.5 knots. The anchorage is protected from all wind directions except northeast. If the wind should pick up from that quadrant, icebergs in Penola Strait can move in and crumple *Northern Light* as easily as if she were built of aluminum foil.

Put the fenders out!
(Rolf)

Soon after we tie *Northern Light* into the middle of the small inlet on Petermann Island, a northbound iceberg gets caught in the eddy at the mouth of our harbor, turns into the inlet, and squeezes against the topsides. From our vantage point it looks like a gigantic king's crown with points 12 feet high.

The iceberg is lovely but threatening. If it presses against us a little harder, our shore lines will snap. If the massive configuration moves astern, it will crumple the windsteering. We could let the shore lines go and allow the iceberg to pass into the bay, but it would return when the tide changes and threaten us from the other side. We hang out a few fenders between us and the iceberg and hope that when the tide changes it will be sucked back out into the channel.

Instead of following the plan we made for it, the iceberg cracks and starts rotating. One half—perhaps 500 tons' worth—rises on its edge, and hooks one of its spires around a port shroud. Fear wells inside me, but I'm helpless to do anything. I can only hope that the ice will not pull down the entire rig. I see that Deborah has turned pale.

The piece begins to push the boat sideways, and for ago-nizing moments the shore lines tighten—until they scream in complaint around the bollard, and the boat slows. Something has to give. Suddenly the big piece of ice hooked on the shroud breaks off and crashes on deck. What remains of the iceberg in the water somersaults, turning in its own radi-us. Miraculously, it doesn't even touch the hull.

Just when we think everything is over and can begin to relax, we hear a piece of ice scraping along the keel and hull on its way to the surface. The sound is terrifying. We hope that the ice will not tear the exposed log propeller away. It doesn't.

After a few minutes the iceberg has disintegrated into a hundred smaller pieces. None can do us any damage, but less than a cable away out in Penola Strait other icebergs are continuously moving past the mouth of our harbor. They are ten… twenty… and yes, hundreds of times bigger than the one that just tangled with us. If the wind increases from northeast such a giant could be blown into our bay and obliterate us. That is if it isn't so large that it gets stuck in the mouth of the bay. If that happens, we'll be well pro-tected but locked in for who knows how long.

96 *Iceberg in tow*

After the experience with the "king's crown" iceberg, we don't care to stand idly when this giant frozen lilypad moves against the hull. Rolf decides on a possible course of action and jumps into the dinghy to try to tow it away. He lassos one arm of the berg and whips his fifteen horses into action. They pull and tug with all their might for ten minutes and go absolutely no-where. However, the ice cowboy sticks to his guns, and eventually the berg begins to move, slowly at first… gathering momen-tum… farther and farther away. Just past the eddy, Rolf releases the rope. The ice-berg continues out into Penola Strait and disappears from sight.

98 The soft light and ever changing hues of pastels color the long dusk in the high latitudes. From our vantage point atop Petermann Island, we look past a penguin rookery to Booth Island.

Payback
(Deborah)

The good weather holds throughout the day, and we treasure every minute. This is our payback—fine weather and a decent anchorage at an island where we can go ashore—it's all we need to begin to recoup the energy spent getting here. Petermann Island provides us with even more. There are two types of both penguins and seals here within sight of the boat, so we can watch the wildlife and at the same time keep an eye on *Northern Light* and the ice.

As soon as Rolf clears the anchorage of troublesome ice, we row our dinghy ashore and land on the rocks. There are some gentoo penguins there, and we plunk ourselves down to watch them waddle down the rocks to go out searching for fish and squid. At the edge they pause and look for evidence in the water of their deadly enemy, the leopard seal. They hang together in groups, conferring with one another, afraid to be the first one in. Suddenly one "accidentally" pushes another—the sacrificial lamb—off a rock and into the water. It's murder if a leopard seal is lurking about.

Rolf and I are enchanted by the penguins' every move. We watch them swimming in groups in the channel, leaping out of the water like porpoises to breathe without losing speed. Then suddenly they appear—like missiles from the sea—and land on their feet on the rocks, above the pounding swell.

We set out to explore the rest of the island, passing a few crabeater seals that have serpentined their mass from the beach to the snow, and fur seals that can walk on land. They are resting there where no indigenous enemy can reach them, oblivious to their surroundings. It is easy to see how simple the sealers' slaughter was.

There are many rocky outcroppings toward the top of the island, and we climb to them and the rookeries. There are thousands of penguins here and they fuss continually at each other. The cumulative effect is so loud that Rolf and I must resort to yelling at each other.

Evening progresses, and the long dusk that leads into sunset at 2300 casts a magical spell. From atop the island, we survey our 360-degree panorama: penguin rookeries, islands, water, ice, fin whales in the channel making top speed to who knows where, mountains... all awash in sunset's colors. We feel blessed. Our arms around each other, we take in one more long sip of the wild surroundings—Antarctica—before descending.

14
Antarctic wildlife

(Deborah)

Polar wildlife is comprised of few species, each with a huge population; penguin colonies can have upwards of 10,000 very vocal members. With necks stretched and bills pointing to the sky, penguins trumpet to attract a mate or to scare off a circling predator. Others honk at neighbors that dare to encroach on their territory. As the intruder struggles to get back to the safety of its own territory, it usually skitters past other nests in the process, setting off a noisy chain reaction.

Since penguins' nests are very close to one another, territorial infractions occur often. Intruders are attacked, sometimes pecked until they bleed. Even for uncoordinated chicks there is no mercy, and for them one infraction usually leads to another. It is a vicious circle; the more frightened the chicks become, the more they dart around through other penguins' territories, suffering continued attacks.

Rookeries are located on rocky areas. The smaller rocks are prized possessions to penguins since they build their nests with them. This important and fairly rare commodity is often stolen, so nests are rarely left unattended. Rocks are so important in a penguin's life that part of the courtship behavior includes the male's ritualistic offering of a rock to the female to begin building the nest. The world over, rocks are a girl's best friend.

99 *We came to look*

99 Rolf's first visit to a penguin rookery atop Petermann Island. He is sitting just outside their territorial limit, and as long as he doesn't stand up, these Adélie penguins don't mind his presence.

100 The Antarctic skua is a predator. It remains close to the rookeries, watching from the snow or the sky for a chance to prey on penguin chicks. A penguin will defend its young against the attack, but since the skua can fly and is much faster on the ground as well, the chick must remain close to the parent to be secure. Should one of the penguin parents die, the chick most likely will perish too, since it is left unprotected when its remaining parent goes fishing.

Skuas also chase other birds, tiring them until they disgorge their catch. The skua is such a fancy flier that it can nab the falling food in a mid-air swoop.

100

101 A gentoo penguin with an orange and black bill sits on its rock nest in which there are one or two eggs. For a month, partners take turns incubating the eggs.

Pairs often return to the same spot to mate. When they meet, a courtship display ensues. First they bow to one another. Then the male turns his bill skyward and with chest heaving in and out, he trumpets. The accepting female returns the display; then, facing each other, they sway back and forth, drawing half circles in the air with their bills.

101

102

102 These Adélie penguins are making their way up the snow-covered hill to the rocks 150 yards above sea level. Their legs are set well back on their bodies, which results in the comical gait we love to watch, but they perambulate quite effectively.

Often, on their way uphill, they lie on their bellies and push with their feet. On the way down, they use the same position to toboggan.

Their wings cannot be folded, nor do they have flight feathers, but the wings do serve as powerful paddles for underwater propulsion.

103 Adélie penguins on their way to fish for krill or larval fish dive in head first. A female elephant seal watches their entry, but since she feeds on fish and squid she poses no threat. The carnivorous leopard seal is another story. When a leopard seal catches a penguin, in one powerful shake it splits the bird wide open (*left*).

104 Three gentoo penguins bask in the sun after fishing. When they first came onshore they lay in the snow on their bellies and scooped up snow to eat. If fresh water is not available, they can drink salt water.

Their webbed feet are used for steering and braking when they swim, and their claws for digging into the snow when they push themselves along on their bellies.

Penguin feathers are short and curved, oily at the overlapping tips and downy toward the skin.

104

105 Penguin chicks are fed by regurgitation. The chick demands food by tapping its bill on the parent's. Adult penguins have pouches in their gullets where they store their catch while they are swimming back from the hunt, so that it is not digested before it gets to the chick.

105

106

106 A gentoo parent and its beanbag-shaped chick. The chick will not moult its downy feathers for about two months, during which time the parents alternate feeding it. The stiff tail feathers can be used for balance while the penguin stands upright.

Note: Penguins often fish in groups, swimming miles to and from fishing grounds at a general speed of 5–10 mph. When they return, they can launch themselves up out of the water onto ice or rocks and land on their feet.

107 *Early morning approach to Lemaire Channel*

Against the light

Nice days feel like vacation; creases ease and wrinkles relax. After a long uninterrupted sleep, Rolf is the first one up this morning. I, under skipper's orders, am to be the queen. Translated, that means that I get to lounge while he prepares a treat for breakfast. The chef's specialty today is a light and crisp waffle made in a heart-shaped Norwegian waffle iron we purchased many moons ago. Steaming coffee, waffles and my choice of toppings... served in bed, while the sunshine streams in through the skylight.

This still, glimmering morning is an opportune time to try to get through the narrow, precipitous Lemaire Channel. Glaciers' tongues end in this channel, so year-to-year, or even week-to-week, it may be congested or blocked with ice. The only way to know if it's navigable is to attempt to pass through it.

Looking north through the crack, we see the high mountains past our destination, Port Lockroy. They look so close that it's hard to believe we won't be there by lunchtime. But they loom across 25 miles of water. We hope that we can make it all the way there and find a secure resting spot before dark.

Early in our approach, Lemaire appears to be jammed with ice pieces, some of which we have seen before, some of which are resting platforms for crabeater seals. The seals barely take notice of us no matter how close we pass to them. Halfway through, and moving by one of the calving glaciers, we are forced to slow to a snail's pace to weave our way through the ice.

In the peak of the whaling period Lemaire Channel was blocked by ice most of the time. As a consequence there are no signs of whalers south of the channel. Lemaire seems to be a border to animals as well; there are no signs that elephant seals have been south of it, and fur seals have only recently been sighted there.

South of Lemaire we were butted against the north-to-south run of the mainland. As we pass out of the dizzying gap, the vista opens to a high archipelago spreading east to west. It is a still day; the sea is dead calm. Antarctica doesn't have the best sailing conditions; there is either too little wind or lots of wind and nasty weather. We are glad we installed an additional diesel tank in Sweden; the extra fuel allows us to motor to Port Lockroy.

This harbor, once used by the Norwegian whaling factories, is one anchorage the Pilot Book does recommend. It is protected in any wind direction save west-to-southwest, when shelter can be taken in a small cove on the west side of the island, as long as the glacier is not calving. The Norwegian eyebolts in the rocks are rusting away, but what is left is still strong enough to hold *Northern Light*'s 14 tons, and we attach a stern line to one of them.

Onshore exploring, we find skeletons of whales that long ago were rendered into oil. The huge bones are whitened but perfectly preserved: vertabrae 1.5 feet in diameter, with blades 5–6 feet high, discs, and jaw bones. Both the setting sun and history cast long shadows across the remains.

108 *Humpback whale in Nimrod Passage*

109 *Evening in Port Lockroy*

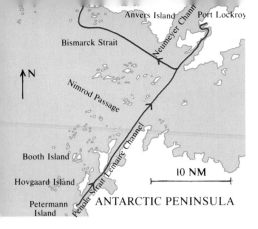

Anvers Island   Port Lockroy
Bismarck Strait
Neumeyer Channel
↑N
Nimrod Passage
Booth Island
10 NM
Hovgaard Island
Penola Strait · Lemaire Channel
Petermann   ANTARCTIC PENINSULA
Island

The weather deteriorates

We leave Port Lockroy and head to Palmer Station to keep a date made over a year ago in Canada. We are to meet the *Lindblad Explorer,* a unique cruise ship, for the third time during our north-to-south voyage. The first meeting was in Svalbard just before our assault on the North Pole pack ice. The second unplanned encounter took place in the Strait of Belle Isle, between Labrador and Newfoundland, while we were both heading toward the anchorage in Red Bay, Newfoundland. We enjoyed camaraderie with the captain, crew and passengers and are eagerly awaiting this rendezvous.

But first, other events and surprises await us at Palmer Station. A U.S. research base, it is filled to capacity for the summer months with scientists and crew from all over the world. More conversation and scientific data is available than is possible for two culture-shocked sailors to absorb, but we tour through each lab and get to have some good ol' plain fun when we can get ashore to talk to the people. And much to our surprise, there are two other yachts there as well. As a matter of fact, there are a total of four yachts in Antarctica this season. The other three are all French steel boats, two of which were built by the same yard that built *Northern Light.*

Our first conversations with the other sailors center around the good weather we have all been enjoying for the last twelve days. We are quite certain that the high pressure that has stalled over the Peninsula will break soon. When it does, it breaks suddenly and fast. From a high of 1010 millibars, it starts to sink 3 millibars an hour, accompanied by a blow. We have tied up *Northern Light* in the middle of the cove with lines to eyebolts in the rocks, and after four hours have to get into the dinghy to double our lines. The station records 50-knot gusts from the northeast. Eventually we are forced to reposition the boat to avoid ice pieces that are snagging on the shore lines and jamming against the hull; the combination could break our lines. We hope that the center of the depression will pass north of us, because if it passes to the south we will get westerly wind, and this anchorage is open to the west near a very active glacier.

The barometer eventually sinks to 973 millibars, the deepest depression we have experienced so far on this voyage. For two days we remain onboard; we can't leave the boat unattended. It is hard to be cooped up on *Northern Light* while the short season dwindles. Finally the wind begins to subside. When it does, scientists and yachtsmen burst into activity around the station.

Adding to the excitement, the *Lindblad Explorer* soon appears and anchors just off the station. In minutes we are aboard the big red ship, renewing old acquaintances and making new ones. The space and comfort is wonderfully refreshing and the camaraderie is perfect for both Rolf and me—Swedish and English are the ship's main languages. Perhaps most unbelievable is that in the inspired belief that we would indeed rendezvous, the *Lindblad Explorer* has brought us mail! It is such a short, sweet visit after so long an anticipation; Rolf and I both smile through tears as the ship departs only hours later.

As the weather stabilizes we have more time in the station. We are able to make some friends and family happy by reaching them on the phone via the ham radio. The scientists tell us about krill and bird behavior, about the Antarctic food chain, and about fish with antifreeze in their blood. They recommend a visit to nearby Humble Island, so we shuttle ourselves there and for the first time observe elephant seals. These live in the midst of a penguin rookery and a giant fulmars' nesting spot, and while we are there the only macaroni penguin we ever see sashays through the rookery.

The next morning, we receive sobering news. A leopard seal was seen attacking some of the station's inflatable dinghies that were tied up as usual to the dock. It punctured and slit several pontoons, but oddly only black and gray ones, ignoring the red boats. We breathe a sigh of relief that there was no one in them at the time and that the dinghies are repairable. But what does this event forbode? Why does the seal attack a dinghy in the first place? Is it a peculiar, isolated incident, or will it be repeated? Would a seal be likely to attack when the dinghy is underway, or will the noise of an outboard engine repel it? Is our red dinghy safe from attack?

112 A female elephant seal watches a male snort and dribble his displeasure at our presence. The largest of the true seals, the male can tip the scales at 9,900 pounds and she at 2,200 pounds. These seals were once hunted for their oil; a third of their weight is blubber. His proboscis is inflatable and was considered a tasty morsel by the sealers.

110 A pair of southern giant petrels on Humble Island rest undisturbed; when annoyed they spray a foul-smelling oil. This bird has a breeding season of 180 days. It lays a single egg which, if lost, cannot be replaced in the same season. The continual drip from its beak provides a method to excrete excess salt.

111 A bevy of beauties: female elephant seals lying in the mud on Humble Island.

110 *Southern giant petrels*
112 *Adult elephant seals*

111 *Young elephant seals*

113 *Be kind to us*
A Weddell seal melts the ice it rests on.

Animal talk

There are times when we pass the animals, and there are times when the animals pass us. It's a simple freedom—one both Rolf and I hope will continue. These seals resting on the ice and digesting their catch are free today from man's hunt, in Antarctica at least. Since the Antarctic Treaty was signed in 1961 seal populations have been increasing, and if the shrimp-like krill, low on the food chain, is not over-fished by man, the seals will continue to flourish.

While we often see seals plowing through the water, nostrils and eyes above the surface, we don't often hear them when we are underway. However, we can hear their very high-pitched, drawn-out noise clearly inside the boat when we are at anchor or becalmed.

The same is true for many other sea birds and mammals we encounter on this voyage; each species has a repertoire of sounds that it makes above and below water. Every time we have been below and heard a new noise, we have rushed on deck to identify its owner. In the process we have learned to identify each by its underwater sounds.

The first experience of this sort occurred while *Northern Light* was becalmed off the coast of Norway. Both Rolf and I were below and heard a series of clicking noises that became progressively louder. We dashed up the ladder and saw several killer whales approaching. The leading whales were using their sonar to identify what was in their path.

The clicking stopped, and a warbling message was passed through the group; then all sound except the noise of their passage through the still water ceased.

Row after row of whales passed us to port, first two, then three abreast, their shiny black-and-white skins glistening. And they kept coming: three abreast, then four and five. We watched them for fifteen minutes. When this "flying wedge" reached seven abreast, it split as they passed us, four to port and three to starboard. For half an hour the pod swam by; there must have been hundreds.

The clicking noise is nearly always the first sound we hear from approaching whales, but they also make hauntingly high-pitched sounds. I wonder if they have given up trying to talk to boats and humans, but sometimes we put on the depthsounder or the cassette deck, since we can't screech out such a high-pitched noise.

We can come close to mimicking a dolphin's squeaky voice, but our vocabulary is too limited to keep their interest. The boat itself seems to be the playmate the dolphins appreciate most. Mid-ocean they often join up with *Northern Light*, hitching a free ride in the bow wave. In decent weather we can watch them from the bowsprit as they swim ahead of the boat.

Light also attracts some creatures. Once in the Roaring Forties, when we were making a nighttime sail change and had a deck light on, a 30-foot Minke whale surfaced just beside *Northern Light*. I was in the cockpit and was startled by the noise of its blow, but I wasn't fast enough to get out of the way of the malodorous spray. I called to Rolf to warn him that the whale was alongside, since I didn't want the whale's loud noise to startle him while working on the fore-deck. The leviathan swam so close alongside that we touched its back. Forty-five minutes later we had to turn the light off to conserve our batteries, and the whale disappeared immediately into the night. How sad we felt not to be able to communicate with it.

I have improved since then—I often talk to the animals, by imitating their above-water noises. I know how to imitate the "auk auk" penguin call that the parent and child make to each other when they surface after a dive. One foolish fledgling actually left the water and tried unsuccessfully to climb a steep bank to reach me. Another that surfaced before its parent did, and got me answering its call, tried to jump into the dinghy. I was surprised that it would mistake me for its mother—penguins must be color blind—I was wearing my international-alert-orange survival suit at the time.

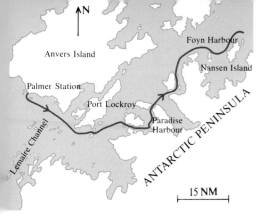

115 *Humpback whale blowing*

A whale of a tale

A mile ahead of *Northern Light* a 45-ton humpback whale is suspended in mid-air. It hangs there for a second, and then instead of sinking back into the water, twists and lands on its back with a resounding smack and an enormous splash.

We have been hoping to see whales up close, and here in the rich feeding grounds of the Gerlache Strait we have spotted duos every few miles. We can head for the humpback showoff even though we have just spent thirty minutes watching a female and her calf, since our selected anchorage is not far away, and the gray weather looks as though it will not worsen.

It is not at all frightening to be around whales in *Northern Light;* we don't believe that they could hole a steel boat. But a few days ago, we were in the dinghy close to an old male, and it was terrifying. Our inflatable is 12 feet long; the whale was 60. Although I did not believe that he would intentionally upset our little rubber boat, I was afraid that he might accidentally capsize it. In warmer climes it would not be a problem, but this water is 28°F, and we were miles away from *Northern Light* in a channel with a 1.5-knot current. Even in our survival suits I didn't like the odds; a manageable risk is acceptable, danger is not.

The first thing we saw of the old male was his tail as he was diving. Rolf wanted to investigate, and we zoomed closer. I felt unsafe near him since there was no way to anticipate where he would reappear, and we did not know if he could sound our rubber craft. So each time he dove, I drove us over to the "protection" of an iceberg, for he could certainly sound that. When he surfaced again, we zigzagged around him and were rewarded with what seemed like liquid gold dripping from his flukes against the setting sun.

Now when we are aboard the big boat we feel no fear, only fascination and pure joy. For two hours the showoff and his mate cavort around *Northern Light,* swimming around and under the dinghy that is being towed astern. Evidently they have no problem sounding it or negotiating their mass around it; not once does a fluke or flipper as much as graze either the inflatable or *Northern Light.*

One whale involves itself with us more than the other. It swims back and forth under the boat. Watching from the spreaders, we see its head to port and its flukes to starboard. Then it comes straight up out of the water just enough for its eye to clear the surface for a good look. Rolf and I are ecstatic; we wave and holler and sing and dance. I

116 Whales can be identified by their diving sequences; humpbacks always raise their flukes before disappearing from view.

117 I experience the thrill of a lifetime when this scarred humpback comes boat-and/or people-watching.

can just imagine the whales talking to each other about what a quiet, pleasant place the Antarctic Peninsula used to be.

I want desperately to touch the whales. The curious behemoth keeps surfacing at the bow of the boat. I stand on the bowsprit and call to it. The humpback pokes its head out of the water again, surveys the situation, and then sinks. After a few minutes I see the water lighten and I know that it will surface again at the bow. Slowly the head breaks the surface. The whale spots me and then begins to rotate. Up and up it rises while extending its 16-foot scalloped, knobby flippers.

The whale is operating blind—the trajectory was computed when sighting me—and it begins to slide away from me just a little too early. I reach out as far as is possible, stretching and straining, but we miss contact by inches. I don't mind; the intent is enough. For me it is the ultimate highlight of the entire voyage, and as long as I live I will smile when I remember this moment.

116 *Humpback dives under the boat*

117 *Perhaps the whale has been hit by a ship*

118, 119 and 120 A 60-foot humpback whale tries for a close encounter. It comes head-first and straight up and out of the water until it sights me, then turns and reaches to me with its flippers, missing me only by inches. I wish that humans would learn to talk to these mammals instead of killing them.

118 *Hello!*

119 *Here I am*

120 *A little closer*

121 Humpbacks are playful behemoths. After surfacing to look at me, this one falls and soaks me with the splash. Smiles, fortunately, are waterproof.

121 *... and this is just the head*

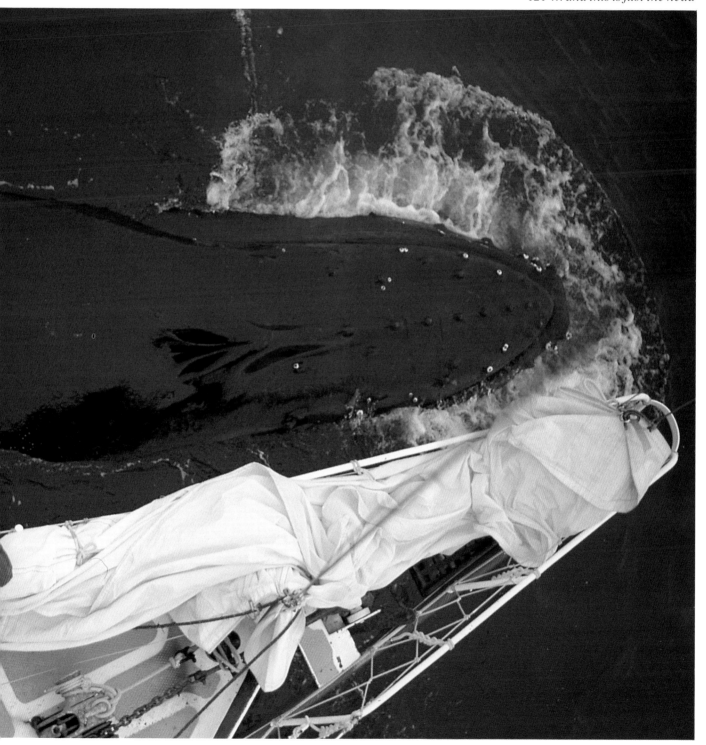

15
Darkening

(Deborah)

122 In Foyn Harbor, we tie up *Northern Light* to the spooky remains of an old whaling ship.

123 I examine the remains of the inflatable dinghy after it was "murdered" by a seal. The lack of a reliable dinghy drastically changes our life and decreases our safety margin.

122 *Foyn Harbor*

Pervading this small bay on Nansen Island is a feeling of death's gloomy spirit. Once a mooring spot for whaling factory ships, it is now filled with the decaying remains of the whaling and sealing industries—an Antarctic cemetery.

The Pilot Book advises that the holding ground in Foyn Harbor is poor and that the wind can blow violently from the exposed southeast sector. But as we approach it we see an opportunity to tie up securely: triangulate mooring lines to eyebolts and take a fourth line to the rail of a half-submerged hulk of a whaling ship. While rowing out one of the shore lines, I cross above the ship's sunken stern. Seeing the wreck beneath the dinghy makes my skin crawl; the slight swell in the bay heaves like a dying breath. Rowing back, I take a more circuitous route.

When *Northern Light* is secure, Rolf and I go exploring in our dinghy. In the next bay we see more evidence of the whalers; their wooden longboats rest high and dry onshore. Sitting amongst the rotting boats are fur seals. From an earlier experience we know that they can be aggressive and can move fast on land, so we don't go ashore.

Back at *Northern Light,* we lift the inflatable on deck for the night as we always do. The following morning Rolf puts it in the water. During breakfast we hear a whooshing sound and rush topside to check for the source. At first we see nothing and hypothesize that it must have been a seal's breathing noise. Then Rolf notices that the dinghy has disappeared; its painter is hanging straight down from the rail.

With some effort he pulls the water-filled remains of our small boat on deck. Each of its five sections has been slashed. Aft of the transom both pontoons are simply gone. The floorboards are floating away. We make no effort to retrieve them; the dinghy is beyond repair. It is so unalterably final, and since there is nothing we can do or anything appropriate to say, we both laugh.

Our assumption is that the damage was done by a fur seal. Fortunately we were not onshore when the attack occurred—or in the dinghy. And we learned our lesson: we'll carry an indestructible, hard dinghy on our next voyage.

But now the fabric of our life is torn too. The dinghy was a crucial piece of equipment; its loss affects us drastically. Although we do have a spare, it is a smaller inflatable for which we have no bracket for the outboard engine; it can only be rowed. From now on, we will not be able to venture far from *Northern Light,* or get ashore in many places.

More importantly, with the loss of the more rugged and stable dinghy a major safety margin has been slashed. We cannot row the spare against much more than 20 knots of wind, and strong wind is more likely to occur as we approach the end of the summer season. In 50 percent of the anchorages left along the Peninsula, shore lines are necessary, yet we may no longer be able to take lines ashore or adjust them when needed. Rolf and I are going to have to be even more aware, prudent and ingenious during the rest of our Antarctic stay.

124 The spacing of a fur seal's front teeth matches the spacing of the slashes, so we believe that such a creature is responsible for the attack on our dinghy. There are two bulls with harems in our anchorage. Perhaps when one bull was in the water he mistook the dinghy's underwater profile for another seal encroaching on his territory, and he attacked to keep the sexy intruder away from his females.

125 These fur seals sit on the beach in front of decaying longboats once used by whalers and sealers. Now protected by the Antarctic Treaty, the fur seal population is increasing after man's ruthless slaughter nearly exterminated the entire species.

Fur seals have external ears, large fore flippers, and hind flippers which turn forward and enable them to walk on land. That ability separates them from the true seals which can only use their flippers for swimming.

123 *Five minutes ago it was a useful dinghy*

124 *Fur seal*

125 *Nansen Island*

126 *Will the visibility last?*

127 *Toward Deception Island*

126, 127 and 128 It is a tense day for us. In Antarctica it takes only a few minutes for very good visibility to be wiped out by dense fog. A few degrees of drop in the air temperature and clouds' undersides lower to rest on the water's surface, making it impossible for us to see either land or icebergs.

128 *Distant fog*

The skipper's privilege
(Rolf)

Late in the afternoon at the entrance to Mikkelsen Harbor on the southern point of Trinity Island, we meet an outgoing current carrying a lot of ice. A deep bay with an active glacier doesn't look too promising as an anchorage, but we find a shoal that the bigger ice pieces can't cross and drop the anchor just behind it.

At just a boatlength to starboard, icebergs drift past continuously. And as close to port is an awash sand bar. Deborah says this can only marginally be called shelter, and I agree; it is barely acceptable and will remain safe only as long as the wind continues to blow from northeast and the current doesn't change.

In the morning the wind is down. But thanks to the current's staying the same, we are still hanging in the slim lane of ice-free water. Out in Gerlache Strait the fog is dense, but in the bay visibility is good. Through a momentary break in the low cover I see wisps of high clouds. The clouds and the fact that after rising all night the barometer is now steady, make me fear that bad weather might be approaching.

What can I anticipate? If a depression tracks south of us we can stay. But if it takes a northerly track, the wind shift will force us to leave this "harbor." If the shift forces us to leave at night, we will find ourselves in a dangerous situation. In this light wind we cannot reach the alternative anchorage at Deception Island before dark. My dilemma is: should we leave an anchorage that is safe now, put out into fog and the presence of icebergs, and risk having to spend the night in a position that can be life-endangering, only because this place *may* become unsafe?

As a skipper I have my precept: seek fact, decide action, and enforce it. To leave safety and definitely expose us to danger in order to avoid an only anticipated but greater danger is the most difficult decision I have ever made. Ten hours later, as we approach Deception Island, it is blowing a 35- to 40-knot easterly gale. This time I was right. But the later the season gets, the more difficult it is to predict the depressions' tracks, and the more the task of skipper/meteorologist begins to resemble a game of Russian Roulette.

16
Ice-free but not trouble-free

(Deborah)

129 *Deception Island bath*

A narrow part of the precipitous crater wall that forms the perimeter of Deception Island is broken down, affording entrance to boats to the inner basin. In we sail, past a high pointed rock, the free-standing sentinel of the channel, searching for our first ice-free anchorage in Antarctica. The narrow entrance channel, "Neptune's Bellows," is true to its name; the wind roars through the funnel in heavy gusts.

We head for Whalers Bay, just north of the entrance. As Rolf is about to release the halyard to drop the mainsail in preparation for anchoring, a gust hits from abeam. As *Northern Light* heels 60 degrees, water pours over the winches into the cockpit. Moments later we are sandblasted by volcanic grit. After the treacherous night we have just spent anchored in an ice field, it seems worthwhile to trade icebergs for cinders. We worry, however, that the gusts screaming down the steep hills may be stronger than the holding the loose bottom affords.

The following morning we are lucky to get a walk ashore, through the ruins of a British base and up to a high overlook called Neptune's Window, before the wind changes direction. When *Northern Light* begins to swing parallel to the beach, we have to seek new shelter and head for the western side of the basin, where a new small-boat harbor was created during the last volcanic eruption, in 1969.

It is a bizarre, barren landscape at the northwestern end, nothing more than volcanic mounds of loose rock and cinder. The mouth of the innermost bay is rather shallow, and there is one other shoal spot inside, but *Northern Light*

130 *Mt. Kirkwood, Deception Island*

131 *Anchored in the inner crater basin*

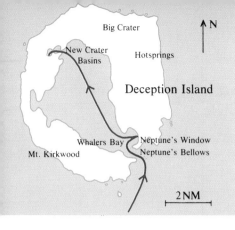

129 Out of my heavy clothes and down jacket, I get a luxurious soak in a steaming hot spring.

130 Deception Island in the western part of the South Shetland Islands is one of the world's largest crater islands. Precipices like Mt. Kirkwood (1,500 feet high) display different compositional strata, notably red brickstone. The ice fields are often hidden by a covering of wind-blown volcanic cinders, making hiking treacherous.

131 and 132 New crater basins were created in the western portion of Deception Island during the 1969 eruption. The innermost basin forms a near-perfect small-craft anchorage, exposed only to northeasterly winds. Reports indicate that its loose sliding sides are filling the bay, and we find that the volcanic deposit does not provide the best holding, but it is a relief to be in the only ice-free anchorage in Antarctica.

makes it in and has plenty of room to swing at anchor.

We hike up the hills surrounding the anchorage to look over the whole basin. We can see some miles down the beach to the ruins of a Chilean station that was destroyed in the last eruption. In front of it the beach is steaming.

Early the following morning, under mild sunshine that warms up the black beaches, we take a lovely, long, leisurely walk to the station. The mixed snow and volcanic vista is bold and magnificent in its natural state, but the burned-out and nearly buried ruins of the station form a desolate scene. Once again man's efforts have been destroyed by nature, humbled by stronger forces.

Along the steaming beach we find two sulphurous hot pools. The first is scaldingly hot, but the second is perfect for a soak. Ah, the pleasure of an unexpected Antarctic hot bath, the first in I won't say how long. I hesitate to get out even when my skin is wrinkled, because I don't relish having to freeze dry... but it turns out that the steam rising from the beach provides a curtain from the wind, and I am comfortable standing naked.

On the return trek we decide to try to find a major crater from the last eruption. We have no map; all we have to go on are memories of pictures a friend showed us. We see a peak that resembles the photo and begin the upward climb toward it. It is difficult at first—we take one step up the cinder slopes and slide back almost as far—but we persevere and finally make it up onto a ridge.

The path ahead is very eroded, as one would expect in a barren, plantless area. Soon we hear running water. The louder the noise gets the more puzzled we become, until we reach the edge of an eroded gully and look down into it to see rushing water. The gully is actually a crevasse and the ridge we have been climbing an ash-covered glacier. Upon further examination we see that there are many layers to this ash-and-snow blanket, each successive layer recording its own wind or snow storm. We retreat hastily in our own footsteps.

Farther up the beach, and after our heartbeats have subsided, we come upon a smooth, ice-free path leading up to the volcano crater. It is an easy climb to the edge where we look down into the crescent-shaped lake. Our heads are filled to overflowing with the day. This feeling of sensory overload has occurred many times during our voyage, so we know the cure: beat a hasty retreat to the known world aboard our floating home, and pull ourselves into our shell to allow it all to settle.

132 *Bird's-eye view of the inner and outer crater basins*

133 *Williwaw-like storm gust in the outer crater basin*

Routine check

(Rolf)

The day after Deborah and I walked to the hot springs, I examine the rigging systematically. Although I don't have to check the lower part of the standing rigging, because I can routinely watch it, I start there. Then I proceed to the wires, fittings, and bolts higher up that I want to inspect before we put out into Drake Passage. I want particularly to examine the stainless-steel heavy-duty strap that connects the forestay to the fixed backstays at the top of the mast.

In Patagonia I found a scratch on that fitting that was either a surface scratch or a hairline crack. To find out if the strap was weakened, I would have had to slacken the rigging, to remove all the instruments at the masttop, and to dismantle the fitting, a difficult job without a crane. If I had loosened one bolt a single thread too much, and the mast had moved the slightest bit out of position, I would never have been able to get the strap back on again, and *Northern Light* would be a sailboat without rigging. The job was too risky to attempt.

I climbed the mast each day for a month to make sure that the "crack" hadn't enlarged. When I saw that it hadn't changed, I judged the whole thing a false alarm and didn't mention anything about it to Deborah. I wanted to be honest with her, but I knew that she was tense facing the prospect of Cape Horn and Drake Passage. She needed all the confidence she could muster to manage what was ahead of us, and I didn't want her to worry needlessly about a possible weakness in the rigging. Although I felt twinges of guilt, I decided to keep quiet.

At the top of the mast in the inner harbor of Deception Island it is a lot windier than down on deck. My eyes water in the cold wind; it is difficult to see properly. To make certain that there is still only a surface scratch on the strap, I slide a fingernail along the suspicious crack. Halfway my nail sinks in. For a few seconds my brain freezes.

When I think about what could have happened had we lost the mast in Drake Passage or here in Antarctica, I am flooded with remorse. At the same time, I feel released. Knowledge sits so much better than uncertainty. The time has ended for agonizing over potential rigging disaster.

When Deborah hears how and when I first spotted the crack and my resultant guilt for keeping it secret, her reaction is far different from what I expect. She believes that I kept a vigilant check on the fitting because I carried the entire responsibility. Shared responsibility often leads to a false feeling of security that ends in catastrophe.

Her insight erases my guilt, and I can begin to channel all

134 *Rolf inspects the rigging*

135 *Will the new strap crack before it takes the right shape?*

136 *What the snow hides...*
137 *Volcanic grit penetrates the sails*

my energy into productive work. Together we look through the dwindling junkyard—now goldmine—under the floorboards in the aft cabin. After a lot of searching we find an old stainless-steel piece which with modification can be used as a replacement strap. After seven hours and as many trips up the mast for measuring, we have manufactured a new fitting. By dusk the only thing that remains is to figure out how to change the cracked fitting for the new one.

When morning comes the weather is more than miserable. The hard cold wind carries volcanic dust and ash, and the dirt is beginning to penetrate the sails, plug up the winches, and black out the deck. In the afternoon the temperature plummets. When it starts to snow I can't work for more than fifteen minutes at a time up the mast; with the windchill factor it is −40°F. It is delicate work, and I cannot wear gloves; my fingers numb. By the time the new strap is in position and I tighten the last bolt, two digits are white and have lost all feeling.

Because the weather continually worsens and we may be forced to move, I tighten the rigging. Only late in the afternoon when all work is finished do I realize how weary I am. I don't feel any hunger; all I can think about is rest. As I descend into the warmth of the boat and close the hatch, I hear the anchor scraping, losing its grip. *Northern Light* is dragging.

138 In Deception Island, I try to row a shore line to the spit on the western side of the inner harbor entrance before dark.

In bad weather land contours fade out. A snowstorm has blocked our view of the mountain on the other side of the outer harbor. At the height of the blizzard the spit also disappears.

In calm weather it is a pleasure to row the small dinghy. Making headway into the wind is another story, and with ice-covered oars and a choppy sea it is practically impossible to row it against more than 20 knots of wind.

138 *Before the storm hits*

139 *Icy decks*

When the wind increases, causing the anchor to drag, we must get a line ashore. The task is more difficult with this dinghy than it would have been with the bigger, heavier inflatable.

We begin with the lighter gray dinghy in the water alongside. As we load the line into the dinghy, the wind flips it upside down. In order not to lose our lines, we must lift the dinghy on deck and load it there.

Because the deck is covered with ice and snow, we move and place each foot carefully. To have either one of us put out of commission by a twisted wrist or ankle would be a disaster in this situation.

Hang on!

(Rolf)

The anchor grabs intermittently. Each time it lets go we drift astern toward the beach. After re-anchoring the second time we hang motionless. But because neither Deborah nor I trust the holding ground, we decide to attach a line to a boulder on the western spit close to the mouth of the inner harbor.

I put every bit of energy I have left into the job. To row against the wind in the little rope-filled inflatable is nearly impossible. In the gusts I hardly make headway. Each wave slops more water—more weight—into the dinghy. When I am not in sync with the sea and slap my oar on a wave, the dinghy immediately turns beam-to the sea, and in mere seconds I lose as much distance as it has taken me minutes to gain. Thinking of my reward, I row as hard as I can to get the line onshore; I must return to *Northern Light* before she starts to drag again and drifts out of the rope's reach. Working at full capacity it takes me over ten minutes to row the paltry 250 feet.

Around 0200 I again hear the wretched rumbling of a dragging anchor. In the dark I can barely distinguish the crater. But from my memory's contour picture I know that we are closer to the beach. A look at the compass shows that the wind has changed from north to northeast. We are swinging in an arc around the boulder I tethered us to; the anchor no longer holds us. If the wind changes another 30 degrees, the rudder will hit the gravel beach.

During the next hour the wind remains steady in direction. Because we never had dinner, Deborah starts to make an early breakfast when she comes on watch. I continue sitting on the ladder looking out through the cupola. Suddenly we are hit by a williwaw-like gust. The boat is thrown sideways. I feel that the rope no longer holds *Northern Light*. As I grab my foul-weather jacket I tell Deborah to preheat the engine, and then I dash out into the cockpit to give full throttle. In the extreme cold it doesn't pay to turn the key to the start position before the fifteen-second preheating is over. I count: 7... 8... 9 seconds as I watch the beach getting closer. An eternity passes.

When the engine starts and I give full throttle in forward, the boat barely gains enough speed to turn her bow back into the wind. She creeps forward at an rpm that in normal conditions would propel her at 6 knots. I keep one eye focused on the line; I don't want it to get caught in the propeller. Once we are upwind of the middle of the bay, I pull

the rope onboard. Deborah comes up on deck dressed in her survival suit, flies to the bow and pumps the anchor aboard.

We know we can't trust the anchor to take hold in the cinder bottom in this wind speed; we must get new lines ashore. But in the gale conditions it is impossible to row upwind to attach the shore lines. Our only chance is to move to the outer harbor, to windward of the eastern spit, where there are bigger boulders we think will withstand the pull of the boat. There, I will drop the dinghy in the water and row a new line ashore while Deborah takes *Northern Light* back to the inner harbor.

While we move slowly forward, we flake two 180-foot lengths of rope into the dinghy as it sits on deck. When we reach the place in the outer harbor where I plan to depart, and while *Northern Light* is practically stationary with her bow to the wind, we lift the dinghy over the side. As we let it go, we see that this plan will not work. The wind is so strong that it creates an airstream around the hull. Even with the weight of the rope, the inflatable flies along the side of the boat like a kite.

A powerful gust hits, lifting the dinghy up to the height of the lifeline. It is about to be flipped over. I throw myself into the rubber boat, hoping that my weight will force the dinghy down into the water so that we will not lose our lines. Against the same gust *Northern Light* loses her forward speed. Deborah dashes to the cockpit, and the engine controls. Although she gives full throttle, she can't stop the boat from turning abeam to the wind. In this position the sea slams the dinghy and fills it with water.

Because *Northern Light* is dragging a water-filled dinghy, she cannot make enough headway to turn the bow back into the wind. I see one more chance. I instruct Deborah to shift to reverse, expecting that this will bring the boat's stern into the wind, where Deborah can stand by while I make ready to row ashore.

Despite full throttle in reverse the engine isn't strong enough to overpower the wind, and we drift slowly toward the eastern spit. Since the plan didn't work, and because the dinghy makes it impossible to power forward with as much speed as we need for maneuverability—without either losing the ropes or ripping the painter from the dinghy—we must get rid of the inflatable immediately.

As I feel the icy water filling up the low boots that I was wearing for standing watch below, I realize that I, dressed in pile clothing, would sink like a rock if the dinghy were to flip. Deborah is already dressed in her survival suit so she

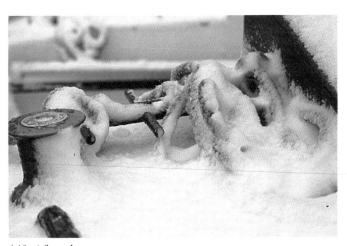

140 *After the snowstorm*
With salt water, we thaw out the ropes that freeze stiff during the snowstorm. The same technique is used on the winches. Had we left the handles in the winches, we could have avoided the extra work.

changes jobs with me. I jump back up on deck and hand her the oars with instructions to row to the eastern spit to attach the shore line.

During this time we have drifted pretty close to the mouth of the inner harbor. With the sea abeam and the wind a little abaft the beam, there is still a chance that Deborah can make it to the spit without being blown past it.

I cannot help Deborah further either now or later if the dinghy should capsize from the seas that continue to smash it from the side. So instead I focus forward on maneuvering *Northern Light* in to the inner crater and gaining the speed that I need to be able to turn her into the wind to meet Deborah on the lee side of the spit.

Before I turn around in the inner harbor, I look back to see that Deborah will not be able to reach solid ground even though she is rowing with all her strength. She misses the spit by 20 feet. But seconds later she sees that the water is shallow enough to stand in, and throws herself out of the dinghy into the ice-cold water. With the sea up to her thighs she slogs ashore, dragging the dinghy and the rope behind her.

She makes it onto the beach. But before she has a chance to pull the dinghy up, the wind howling around the point grabs it. Even though the inflatable is weighed down with both rope and water, it capsizes. The rope ends up in the

water. I worry that if Deborah lets go of the dinghy to take care of the lines first, the dinghy will blow away. Without a moment's hesitation, she continues across the snow-covered cinders to a rock where she can secure the dinghy. Then she disentangles the mess of shore lines, secures an end around a huge boulder with a bowline, flakes the rest into the dinghy, launches it, and jumps in.

Meanwhile, as soon as I arrive in the lee of the peninsula from which Deborah departed, I turn *Northern Light* around and head back for the point where I expect she will drift in the dinghy. Oars shipped, she brakes the dinghy's speed by feeding out the rope slowly so that the dinghy cannot "sail away" in the storm gusts. When we finally intersect she uses all her remaining strength to grab *Northern Light* and hold on.

As soon as I belay the end of the shore line that Deborah hands me and she is onboard, I help her bring the dinghy ondeck. She sums up the entire experience with a soft "wow."

When I stop the engine, the strain on the line is so heavy that it runs from the boulder to the bollard without ever touching the water's surface. It is stretched so tightly that it feels like a steel wire. In the wind's push, we hang so steadily on the shore line that for the first twelve hours, we don't even bother dropping an anchor. As the depression center passes, the barometric pressure reaches our new record low of 964 millibars. When the wind temporarily decreases, we drop the anchor and double up the shore line. Only instead of rowing we now pull ourselves along our rope. It is a lot simpler.

141, 142 and 143 Snow and ice on ropes is beneficial in one way: it reduces chafe. Attaching the second shore line, I make sure that the shackle is positioned exactly at the pulling point. I wear neoprene diving gloves while working in the extreme cold.

Because we expect a new wind increase after the center of the low passes, we double up our shore lines during the "lull." Now instead of rowing we pull ourselves along the already attached rope.

Each time the tide ebbs, it moves the lines to the "wrong side" of rocks on the shoreline. To avoid chafe, we move them back at each low tide.

141 *Doubling shore lines on the eastern spit*

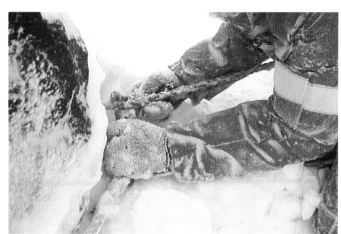

142 *Icy covering reduces chafe*

143 *Toward rest*

17
Brushstrokes in black and white
(Deborah)

144 *North, following Livingston Island*

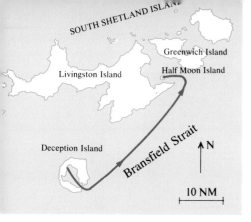

144 On a glorious day, *Northern Light* is underway in the Bransfield Strait, between the Antarctic Peninsula and the South Shetland Islands. We sail close to Livingston Island to get a good look.

Just before we pass through Neptune's Bellows to leave Deception Island, Rolf sets sail. As the mainsail rises, snow and ashes fly out of the folds onto the deck and into our eyes. Every crease in the sails is marked with a black line. There is no way for us to get the abrasive grit out, and I can practically hear the fibers being chafed.

The west wind gives us a glorious downwind sail in Bransfield Strait. As the mainsail fills, its belly presses against the shrouds and the black ash caught between the strands of the stainless-steel wires transfers to the sailcloth. It is an ugly souvenir—one we will carry with us as long as the sail lasts. Worse is the potential damage; I make a silent note to myself to set aside some future time for repairs.

We keep to the northern side of the channel to get a good view of the other South Shetland Islands as we glide past. Our spirits are high because of the favorable wind direction; downwind is a free ride. I enjoy my time at the wheel and think back to the many miles we spent in this same sort of cool and slightly sunny weather when we were in the Patagonian Channels.

While we are underway Rolf fine-tunes the rigging that was slackened during the replacement of the masthead fitting, and we gybe back and forth several times to accommodate his work.

Ahead we see another yacht just on the horizon. She is most likely heading to King George Island too, and we continually gain on her. But suddenly a huge pod of killer whales, their tall fins unmistakable, appears on our port side. We decide to follow them, quickly drop sail, turn on the engine, and power in their wake around the eastern side of Livingston Island until they simply disappear.

In their place our curiosity is tweaked by the odd, craggy landscapes of the nearby islands. There are many needle-like rocks and pinnacles, as there are outside the perimeter of Deception Island, but these appear broken down, shattered and covered by colorful lichens. A quick check on the chart reveals that one of the smaller islands in sight—Half Moon Island—has a likely anchorage, so we head in to check it out.

As the wind is westerly, we are sheltered nicely in the crescent-shaped bay. The beauty of the one side that is steep-to, crowned with rock pillars and occupied by chinstrap penguins, is enough to make us stay for a while. It should be a good spot to spend time onshore while we wait for the proper weather cycle to pop out into Drake Passage on our homeward journey.

In the late afternoon fishing time begins, and one-third of the penguin population heads offshore. Their raucous hue and cry billows off the island as they waddle down from the rookeries on high ground. By chance we are anchored in the middle of a major path, and *Northern Light* is suddenly surrounded by thousands of "auking" chinstraps; the water boils as they porpoise around the boat.

There are lots of seals in the water as well, and we witness a gory scene as a leopard seal nabs a chinstrap for dinner. The other penguins streak away in all directions. Through the binoculars we see that there are plenty of fur and crabeater seals onshore. We want to go for a walk before dinner, but remembering the fate of our red dinghy, I have to ponder whether or not I am willing to travel the short distance to shore in the little gray dinghy. My adrenalin is pumping as Rolf rows.

But what treasures there are ashore! It's getting late in the season and the young of every species are maturing. The young fur seals are very active; they charge at one another and chase each other into the water. The penguin chicks are moulting their downy feathers. What a comical sight they are with patches of fluffy down left in clumps. Especially funny looking are those who have moulted all but their head feathers; they look as though they are sporting spiked toupees. Near the chinstrap rookery at the top of the hill under the shadow of the pillars is a bird that we haven't seen before: the small white sheathbill and its chick. It is a scavenger and feeds on whatever it can steal from other birds or seals. While the parent is away, the unafraid chick accompanies us around the rookery.

During the night the barometer rises above 1000 millibars for the first time since the high pressure prevailed over the Peninsula a month ago. We enjoy a rare star-filled sky, and a little before midnight it actually rains. This is probably the last nice weather of the season, and seasons in the Polar regions are more apt to change abruptly than gradually.

Within four hours the barometer begins its descent, and the wind shifts. We alternate anchor watch throughout the night, but only gusts sweep in the mouth of the harbor from the northeast, and we are not forced to leave the anchorage in the dark.

We get another day onshore amidst the seals and penguins. But when the sky becomes more and more overcast and ominous looking, we hightail it back to *Northern Light*. During the rest of the afternoon the wind increases, but it remains constant from the west, leaving us in shelter. Both of us decide to go to sleep early and get some rest.

After midnight I wake up because of a weather change—

the wind is dying. It is time to stand anchor watch, so I dress and move to the navigation station, light the kerosene lamp, and sit there drinking a cup of tea. When I hear the first traces of wind rattling the halyards, I begin the next step in the vigil: recording instrument readings every fifteen minutes: barometric pressure, wind direction, and depth under our keel.

The first time that the wind moves around to the northeast and our anchorage becomes exposed, I wake Rolf. Seconds later a small bergy bit hits the hull. We decide to preheat the engine and start it in case the wind doesn't shift back. As the engine turns over and comes alive the first heavy gust hits us. We hear the anchor chain strain. It is time to move.

We don foul-weather gear and climb up on deck as quickly as possible. The wind is still increasing. We will not be able to communicate reliably with each other by voice because of the wind's howl. So, as much as we hate to lose our night vision, we turn on the spreader lights to facilitate hand signalling. I take the wheel and engine controls, Rolf heads for the bow. He kicks the chain out of the chock and begins to pump up the anchor. With signals long ago formalized, Rolf directs: forward... stop. Forward...

I can tell that he is straining more than just against the wind. With the next hand signal, Rolf instructs me to power to starboard and I realize what is amiss: the anchor chain is caught on something. I turn the wheel. The maneuver doesn't work. I can feel that the boat is being held in the clutches of an underwater monster, and on Rolf's signal I ease off the throttle before the chain snaps.

All the while the wind is intensifying, and a whole channel's worth of ice is moving in on us. Ice, too, could break the chain; we have to get out of here fast. Rolf signals me to swing the boat around to port. I'm sure we are both hoping the same thing: that the chain is only wrapped once and that it will come free this time. Otherwise we are going to have no choice but to cut the anchor loose and leave it and a good portion of our chain behind.

I circle *Northern Light* around in a rather big loop to port while Rolf lets out chain. He signals: engine in neutral. When the boat stops, he motions me ahead slow. He continues to pump at breakneck speed... and continues... and continues—we are free. Rolf secures the anchor and meets me in the cockpit. It begins to snow. There is no moonshine, no starshine, and neither navigational lights nor beacons to aid us.

A glance and a nod later, I go below to the navigation desk. I turn off the spreader lights and plot our course to the northern point of Half Moon Island; then I give Rolf a compass course. We can't wait for his eyes to adjust to the pitch black. While he struggles to see ice in a snow-filled gale, I watch the depthsounder, double checking to the depths marked on the chart and making sure that he is staying on course. I also watch the log and record the mileage so that I can tell him when to alter course. Flying blind, operating on instruments only, I am very happy that we are so familiar with the equipment, and that I know for example that the log overreads by 10 percent. Not knowing could mean making our turn too soon and ending our voyage on the rocks.

It is a tense time and we must act clearly, decisively and accurately. Our lives depend on it. There is no time for reflection; we each have a job to do. Neither of us can help the other and we both must trust one another to do the job. Rolf has snow and ice-cold spray stinging his face in a bitter cold wind and must maintain a vigilant watch for ice while steering. I have to work with figures, and I can't afford a single arithmetic mistake.

Each successive minute passes without the sickening sound of *Northern Light*'s hitting a final piece of ice. We make it around the northern end of Half Moon Island and proceed 3 miles in the relative calm of the lee to the chosen spot where we lie ahull until morning's light. We both win the bet this time: first light shows that we are just where we thought we were, just where we wanted to be.

146 Just before weighing anchor Rolf kicks the anchor chain out of the chock. When the boat is anchored the chock rather than the windlass takes the strain of the pull of the anchor.

147 Underway during the forced nighttime maneuver, I remain below to plot a course and to watch the depthsounder and log. I continually shout up to Rolf the course to steer while he watches for ice in a blinding snowstorm and steers *Northern Light* into the relative calm of the lee.

145 *Leaning to reach the throttle*
146 *Readying to trip anchor*

147 *Course 43°, Variation −13°, Deviation +3°*

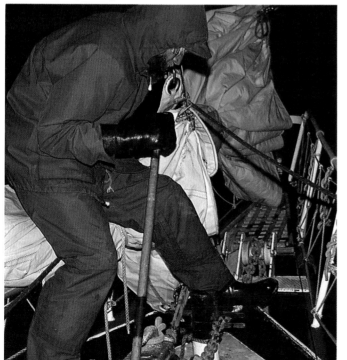

148 *Last anchorage in Yankee Harbor*

Expectations
(Rolf)

In the northeasterly wind we move to Yankee Harbor and toward the glacier wall that rims the inner bay. The bottom is very rocky and uneven, and there are cracks into which the anchor may very likely slide and remain. Only because we have no alternative, we let go the anchor in 30 feet of water and hope for the best. Deborah and I now have nothing to do but wait for the wind to change to southwest so we can get underway toward the Falkland Islands.

The positive aspect of the bay is that it is nearly ice-free. Only on occasion does the glacier rumble and calve. Sometimes the boat rolls so that it is difficult to rest or cook, but the motion doesn't bother us. The time in Antarctica has given us a new view about what constitutes an acceptable anchorage. As long as the boat is safe, we have a good time. If the wind roars in the rigging, we just increase the volume on the tape player.

The next day enough snow blows off the glacier to plug the dorade air vents. Even though we have the companionway hatch open slightly, it gets very damp inside the boat. For the first time since we came to Antarctica, condensation runs in rivulets down the portholes and hatches.

No music in the world can alleviate this woe. Besides, I am pretty bored with our tapes. So I go on deck to make an inspection. Even though it's snowing, I feel better outside than below in the damp cold. I walk around slowly, touching the shrouds to make sure they have the right tension, spinning the winches to make sure they have not frozen, when my eye catches a tiny corrosion stain on one of the running-backstay blocks. Upon examination, I see that the stainless-steel strips running on each side of the block have cracks. When I check the corresponding strips on the other side of the boat, I find cracks in them too.

This is the second time in a week that I have discovered weakened stainless parts just in time to avoid the disastrous consequences of rigging failure. In the last six months, besides the cracked stainless pieces, we have changed two shrouds and one forestay, all of which were over-dimensioned on purpose. While manufacturing new stainless-steel parts for the blocks, we discuss the higher-than-anticipated amount of wear and tear our gear has suffered. We conclude that probably the high-frequency vibrations from the oft occurring roar in the rigging combined with the cold have accelerated the aging process.

At dawn on the fourth day in Yankee Harbor the wind changes to westerly. Low clouds rush a few hundred feet above the masthead; the visibility is good only close to the water's surface. If we hadn't been waiting so long for fair winds to leave Antarctica, we probably would have re-anchored in a more protected spot and waited for better visibility.

We look at the rocks onshore and see that it will soon be

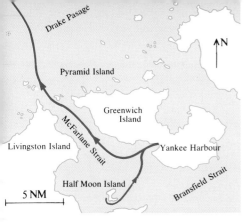

high tide. This means that if we get underway now we can pass through the McFarlane Strait at slack water, the prerequisite for even considering such a narrow route. After experiencing the force of the tidal stream in the Gulf of Coronados in Chile, we can imagine how the water will boil when an outgoing tide sets against the sea that remains in Drake Passage after last night's storm. We will not risk such turbulence.

If we can go out through McFarlane Strait, we can count on being far enough north before dark to be beyond the greatest ice danger. If the tide is not in our favor, the alternative route out is around King George Island where we would certainly have to spend a night amongst icebergs. The advantage to the former alternative is clear as long as we don't realize too late that we are caught in a tide rip's breaking sea.

Three exciting hours of sailing pass before we reach the first shoals at the eighth-of-a-mile-wide entrance to the passage and can get an indication of the direction of tidal set. In the fair southwesterly wind we sail fast and have only a few minutes to judge the current. No matter what we measure it against, we can't distinguish its direction, and a couple of nervous minutes follow. Shall we continue on or turn around and go back to Yankee Harbor?

A few minutes later we are out into Drake Passage. A castle-sized iceberg that we pass at a distance of a quarter of a mile disappears on and off behind the mountainous waves. But the sea doesn't break dangerously the way it would had the tide been outgoing. I release a deep breath. Even this final time we have managed to be in tune with nature's cycles.

It is March 10, and we are sailing away from Antarctica. We will see dolphins again soon when we cross the Convergence, and the color green not long after, in the Falkland Islands.

In two months of sailing time, 8,000 homeward-bound nautical miles will pass under *Northern Light*'s keel. The weather will get warmer until it is hot. We plan to have a special celebration every time we can discard another layer of well-worn clothing… and ceremoniously drop it over the side.

All of this carries us toward new excitement: a time of meeting cherished family and friends we haven't seen for two years, to listen to their stories, and to tell ours. We look forward to sharing our many-faceted adventure and to planning the next one.

149 *Outward bound*

When *Northern Light* passes Pyramid Island we can distinguish only the lower part of its steep sides. The 640-foot-high peak is obscured by the low ceiling.

It is our last Antarctic landmark. We are out. There is no return; in the poor visibility it is impossible to navigate from the sea back through the shoals. Less than ten minutes later we no longer see land.

What we wish for now is for the southwest wind to hold long enough for us to get sea room in Drake Passage before the wind shifts back to northwest and increases.

Our hat is off to the best of human characteristics. Respect and kindness and generosity of spirit were the most valuable resources generated onboard Northern Light and gratefully accepted from the outside world. These qualities, more than anything else, made this voyage a success.

The Antarctic is the earth's kidney, a purification system for the entire world. Taking care of the internal health of the planet is the base for our continuing existence. Let's protect Antarctica. Let's declare it a nature and wildlife preserve—a park for survival. Let it be left for all, with no national claims.

Technical information

(Rolf)

Northern Light is a 40-foot, 14-ton, double-ended, steel ketch with a 5′8″ draft, designed by Jean Knocker, built by META, Tarare, France, in 1973–74.

Hull, deck and superstructure: The U-section keel is 1″ on the bottom and ⅝″ on the sides. The lowest hull plate is ⅓″ thick. The next is ¼″, and the topsides are ⅙″. Deck and superstructure are ⅛″-thick steel. Frames and beams are ¼″ by 2 ½″ spaced 21″ apart. The ten tie-rods joining the deck beams and floors are 3″ by ⅓″-thick angle irons. Permanent ballast is 7,700 lbs of steel and ferrocement, and trim ballast is 1,100 lbs of 88-lb lead pigs.

Anti-corrosion treatment: Sand blasted and cold zinc treatment on outside and inside. Tar epoxy coating in the bilge. Outside finishing treatment: International 708. Underwater: Micron 25.

Interior and insulation: All frames and beams are sistered with non-structural wood frames. The main bulkheads are bolted to the steel frames and beams. The interior is removable in sections so that we can inspect the hull. Between the 2″-thick styrofoam insulation and the hull is ½″ air space for circulation inside each frame section.

Through-hull fittings: 3″ steel pipes are welded to the hull, ending above the waterline. Seacocks and hoses can be changed without hauling the boat.

Heater: Wallas 3000, kerosene. Reflex diesel, in case we had to winter-over in the polar regions.

Tanks: Water: 100 gallons, sufficient for two people for fourteen weeks. We have a rain catcher to replenish tanks. Diesel: 105 gallons, sufficient for 120 hours at 6 knots. Kerosene: 40 gallons, sufficient for eight to ten months cooking and light.

Ventilation: Dorade vents, with air/water separators, are adjustable and can be fully sealed from belowdecks.

Stove: Taylor kerosene, two-burner, with oven. Spare: single-burner Primus.

Toilet: Vacuum principle, no valves to open or close and 100 percent leakproof. Main valve closed in heavy weather.

Bilge and working pumps: Three Whale Gusher 10s for fore-and-aft bilges, holding tank, and toilet. Filters added before bilge pump.

Hatches: Goiot.

Engine: Perkins 4–108 lowline, which with fixed three-blade propeller makes maximum speed of 7.75 knots, and can make steering speed against 70 knots of wind in sheltered sea.

Electric system: 12-volt alternator, 45 amp/hour. Separate batteries for starter engine and lights. Solar cells, 20 amp/day in tropics.

Rigging: Mast and booms: Marco Polo aluminum. Masts are stepped on deck. Climbing steps in both masts. Turnbuckles: Lewmar bronze. All halyards are wire to rope tails. Spare halyards are rope. Main topping lift can replace the main halyard. Standing rigging: ¹⁄₁₉-strand stainless-steel wire, with Hasselfors swedge fittings. Wire dimensions: Mizzen—all stays and shrouds are 7 mm, running backstays are 6 mm. Main—forestay and inner forestay are 10 mm, double backstays are 9 mm, upper and lower shrouds are 9 mm, lower shrouds are 8 mm, running backstays are 9 mm.

For the first 65,000 miles *Northern Light* was sailed with side-by-side double forestays. During that time, strands broke in two forestays. North ice to south ice, the boat was sailed with a single 10 mm forestay, to increase tension and improve the boat's windward performance. After 20,000 miles, strands broke in the top.

Reef system: Slab reef. Booms have one reef winch on each side, making it possible to work on the windward side. Nylon webbing through the grommets in the luff have a stainless-steel ring on each end. The rings are easier to hook onto the reef hook on the boom than the grommet itself. No slides have to be released from the mast track when the sail is reefed.

Windsteering: Atoms. Servo-pendulum principle. Windsteering lines attach to a chain that is 1 ½ ft long. The chain attaches to a hook at the forward end of the tiller. We move it link by link to compensate for the boat's weather helm. With the boat "fingertip-trimmed," the windsteering has a very easy job. It steers the boat on all points of sail, and no storm has so far forced us to hand steer. Down to 1 knot speed, the windsteering keeps *Northern Light* on course. The wheel is released when the windsteering is in use.

Ground tackle: Two 45-lb CQR plow anchors and a 35-lb high-tensile Danforth anchor. One CQR is permanently attached to 225 feet of ½″ chain. The bitter end of the chain is attached belowdecks with rope to an eye in the chain locker. When the chain is all out the rope is visible just underneath the capstan and can be cut in an emergency.

Windlass: Simpson-Lawrence hand-powered.

Sheet and halyard winches: Goiot, Gibb and Lewmar.

Sheets: Herman Gotthardt.

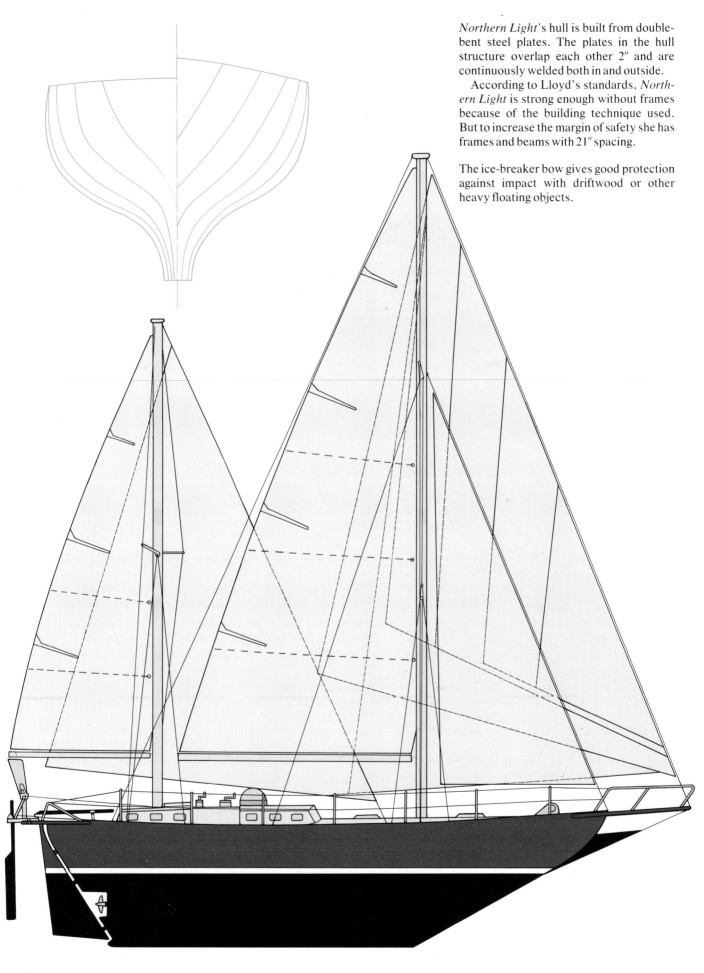

Northern Light's hull is built from double-bent steel plates. The plates in the hull structure overlap each other 2″ and are continuously welded both in and outside.

According to Lloyd's standards, *Northern Light* is strong enough without frames because of the building technique used. But to increase the margin of safety she has frames and beams with 21″ spacing.

The ice-breaker bow gives good protection against impact with driftwood or other heavy floating objects.

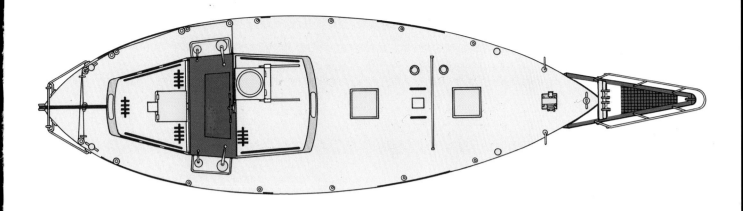

Designer	number	sail	ft²	cloth-weight gsm	cloth
Lidgard	1	main	330	350	US Dacron
(N. Zealand)	1	mizzen	150	350	US Dacron
	1	staysail	140	350	US Dacron
Elvström	1	genoa I	450	230	Bainbridge
(S. Africa)					
Syversen	1	main	330	350	Hood
(Sweden)	1	mizzen	150	350	Hood
	1	yankee I	430	240	Hood
	2	yankee I	300	300, 250	Hood
	1	genoa II	300	300	Hood
	2	working jib I	220	350	British Terylene
	1	working jib II	130	400	Hood
	1	storm jib	65	400	Hood
	2	storm jib	65	300	British Terylene
	1	mizzen staysail	350	200	US Dacron

Every sail panel has three seams: one white and two blue or brown. The color threads have lasted longer. Most headsails have Wichard snap hanks which can easily be attached or released with one hand. We found them superior to the old brass piston hanks especially when we were wearing mittens in the cold. We did not find any abnormal wear from the Wichard hanks on the forestay.

Compasses: Neco repeater with the compass in the mizzen 10 feet above deck. Maximum error from Northern to Southern Hemisphere is 3 degrees. At the navigation desk, the spare Sestral Major is surprisingly correct, considering its proximity to the steel hull. Heeling deviation is big and difficult to determine close to the Poles. I make regular deviation checks by taking amplitude.

Logs: VDO Sumlog. Walker tow log, as spare. Sumlog made the entire voyage without needing a new steel cable. The ice broke 2 ½ of the 3 blades from the log propeller. Even so, it only underread by 10 percent.

Sextants: Freiberger and cheap plastic spare. To get star sights, it is necessary to change mirrors every second year.

Additional navigation equipment: Sailor/Radio Holland radio direction-finder with a cross loop in the top of the mainmast. The equipment itself is very reliable, but radio direction-finding as a navigation aid has too many built-in errors to be reliable. Shipmate satellite navigator: Even though we had been warned that the too-frequent satellite passes over the Pole would lead to unreliable fixes in Antarctica, we got regular and reliable fixes.

Personal protection against the wet and cold: Foul-weather gear by Henri-Lloyd with built-in safety harness in the jacket. Rubber boots: Norwegian fisherman hi-tops. Hi-top rubber mittens, with inner woolen mittens. Neo-

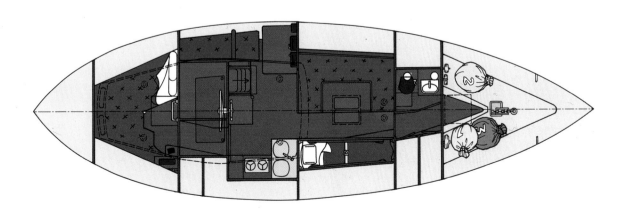

prene diving gloves. We liked rubber mittens for long tricks at the wheel, but for sail handling the diving gloves keep hands warmer and make it easier to tie knots on reeflines.

Under foul-weather gear: Layers: cotton underwear, then Patagonia pile jacket, pants and socks, then fiberfill vest or wool sweater and cotton or synthetic pants. During heavy deck work, we wear a minimal barrier of warm clothes under our foul-weather gear. The key is not to work up a sweat in too-warm clothing, which results in getting cold.

First aid: We have everything on board from antibiotics to dental equipment. During the entire voyage we only used 2 Band-Aids.

Amateur radio: Kenwood TS 120S, N1BHI/MM tuner, Ham Key manual key, vertical T antenna configuration, capacitive top hat strung between masts, dual forward and reverse power meter.

Food: Northern Light is not outfitted with a fridge or freezer. Even so, we are never lacking for fresh food. In addition to our fresh supplies, we always carry at least three months' worth of spare provisions, in case the passage takes longer than anticipated.

Foods that last more than a year: dried beans, rice, noodles, flour, dry yeast, grains, milk powder, dried fruit, nuts, sprouting seeds, freeze-dried soups. A yoghurt culture can be kept alive indefinitely and from yoghurt, we make cream cheese. It can be spiced et voilà, home-made boursin.

Long-lasting fresh supplies: potatoes, pumpkins, squash, onions, cabbage, beets, carrots, citrus fruits, and green apples. Eggs stay fresh 40–100 days, depending upon storage temperature. Cheese can be stored a month, by covering it with vegetable oil.

The first days at sea we eat mainly fruits and vegetables of limited shelf-life. Throughout the voyage canned meats, vegetables and fruits are used as ingredients in dishes. We use no "heat it 'n' eat it" canned products.

We do not generally take vitamins, but did use a supplement during the South Ice segment of our voyage.